MW01204954

Gifts *of* Grace

DEB MARCOTTE

Debra F. Marcotte
Phil 4:13

WestBow
PRESS
A DIVISION OF THOMAS NELSON

allie

WestBow Press books may be ordered through booksellers or by contacting:

WestBow Press
A Division of Thomas Nelson
1663 Liberty Drive
Bloomington, IN 47403
www.westbowpress.com
1-(866) 928-1240

Because of the dynamic nature of the Internet, any web addresses or links contained in this book may have changed since publication and may no longer be valid. The views expressed in this work are solely those of the author and do not necessarily reflect the views of the publisher, and the publisher hereby disclaims any responsibility for them.

Any people depicted in stock imagery provided by Thinkstock are models, and such images are being used for illustrative purposes only.

Certain stock imagery © Thinkstock.

ISBN: 978-1-4497-6445-6 (hc)
ISBN: 978-1-4497-6446-3 (sc)
ISBN: 978-1-4497-6447-0 (e)

Library of Congress Control Number: 2012915168

Printed in the United States of America

WestBow Press rev. date: 09/13/2012

Acknowledgements

Special Thanks to Brent Youngs who turned this story into a masterpiece.

Thank you to the countless friends who line and content edited the book.

I am most grateful to God who called me to tell the story so that others

would have hope, and that He would be glorified.

PROLOGUE

A mother will speak many phrases about her children during the course of her life. In 2008, Deb Marcotte lived a parent's worst nightmare as she uttered these words regarding Allie, her four year old daughter: *I think she's had a stroke.* As Deb spoke these terrifying words to her husband, the reality of the moment began to sink in; a reality that no parent should ever have to endure.

Deb and Donald knew that something was not right but as good parents, they always wanted to believe that their children were safe and healthy. The fact is four-year old Allison, Allie for short, had been limping on her right leg for three days. But on this day, while attempting to paint Allie's fingernails, Deb realized that Allie couldn't lift her right arm. Allie didn't wince in pain at the multiple attempts; she simply could not move her arm. Donald began to cry as he watched. Deb hugged her husband and quickly gathered Allie. The drive to the doctor's office would be only thirty minutes, yet it was the beginning of an unbelievable journey of turmoil for the Marcotte family. Unexpected and unexplained medical conditions would haunt them for years with few silver linings showing up in the darkest of clouds. It would be enough to destroy any family, to exhaust the physical and spiritual capacity of any mother. Deb would struggle but through it all she maintained her prayers, maintained her love and appreciation of God and faced all of these daunting struggles with her faith in check.—Brent Youngs

CHAPTER 1

—❧❀❧—

Donald and I began our life together in a small, rural Oklahoma community called Tiawah. Donald had purchased 110 acres of land through an auction just before we were married in December of 1992. Speckled with a few modest homes, farms and ranches with miles of rolling hills and green pastures, tiny Tiawah is nestled into the outer edges of Claremore, in northeastern Oklahoma. Tiawah was the perfect location for us to begin a family while staying slightly removed from the crowds and traffic of Tulsa. I had finished my Bachelor of Arts at the University of Tulsa but continued to drive four hours to Stillwater and back, three times a week, to finish my Master's degree at Oklahoma State University. I then began working as a Child Development Specialist for the State Department of Health's Soonerstart program. What I wanted more than anything was a family.

Throughout my life, I had prayed to God for a myriad of issues, ideas and possessions. This time, I prayed that God would bless me with a baby. I promised Him that I would be a good mother. It was a difficult road, but God provides in His time; something I learned to never question. Donald and I were married six years before God blessed us with our first born son on March 17, 1998, the day our lives would change forever. We were so happy; happy and ignorant of what challenges lay ahead. Like most new parents, we were sure that our child was going to be the smartest and most handsome child on the planet. He was eight pounds, five ounces of perfection; untouched by the world and imperfect parents. No mistakes had been made . . . .

1

yet. He was by far the biggest baby in the nursery, a fact my husband proudly shared with everyone. My husband, Donald, a man who sees the world from a five-foot eight-inch frame was elated that he was a big boy. We named him Brennan, the name that his daddy and I agreed on after dismissing some non-negotiable options such as Hercules, Mustang Henry and Thor.

Behold, children are a heritage from the LORD, the fruit of the womb a reward. Like arrows in the hand of a warrior are the children of one's youth.—PSALM 127:3

Brennan Matthew was a gift from God to Donald and me. But the gift came with an unexpected beginning. Brennan entered the world blue, limp and breathless. He was immediately rushed to the Neonatal Intensive Care Unit, NICU, of St. Francis Hospital in Tulsa, where he remained for the first 45 minutes of his life. Through God's grace and the attentive care of the hospital staff, he quickly progressed into the beautiful boy who glowed in his father's image and was the favorite among the nursery attendants. I knew my prayers had finally been answered and I prayed that God would give me the guidance to raise young Brennan in the way that He intended. But as most new, young parents soon learn, the untold joys and challenges of child rearing begin immediately after waving goodbye to the hospital nurses.

Brennan was a terrible sleeper; he had colic. I would hold him all night while he slept on my stomach. The pressure helped relieve his gas pains. In fact, because he had trouble sleeping and I was breastfeeding him, it was easier to just keep him in bed with me. His father chose to move out of the bedroom not long after Brennan was born. The baby, he said, made too much noise and he needed his sleep because he had to go to work in the morning, unlike me. I stayed home and as far as Donald was concerned, I could sleep whenever the baby slept; which wasn't often. Brennan also battled with laryngomalacia, as a baby. It was caused by his larynx being too floppy. Therefore, when he cried, he sounded distinctly like a donkey—*eeeehaw*. Thankfully, he outgrew that before we considered soundproofing his room. But between colic, his unrelenting gas pains and his perfect donkey impersonation, I'm amazed that any of us got any sleep. Brennan also had projectile vomiting. This is a phenomenon that only a few fortunate parents get to experience. It is slightly digested milk, or in some cases formula, that literally explodes from the child's mouth with enough force to hit the opposite wall, unless, of course, an unfortunate person happens to be holding this child. The first time we experienced it, we just stood, mouths agape, shocked that our son had enough force in his tiny body to produce such a violent explosion of semi-digested milk. But to me he was still perfect.

We were far from perfect as parents. As Brennan developed from helpless infant to toddler, we began to build a list of parental mistakes that we had promised we wouldn't make. Our first mistake, at least the first to be recorded in the baby book, was introducing fruit baby food before vegetables. I was aghast the day his daddy fed him bananas before he had finished trying all of the vegetables. The books told us to introduce vegetables before fruits. Being a devoted reader of all parenting and child-rearing books—I adhered tightly to written words which promised to produce a healthy, handsome, good citizen of the United States. I unleashed what was the first of many blind furies on the man who had made this horrible mistake. It was as if he had totally ruined my perfect baby, my perfect world. Donald was certain that I had lost my mind, or at the very least, given new definition to the role of overprotective parent.

Mistake number two, as recorded in the baby book, was when Brennan got his hands on the lawnmower keys at two years old. He threw them with all his might over a fence and into the three-foot high grass where our cattle grazed. My reaction to the banana fiasco was child's play compared to my husband's reaction to the lost lawnmower keys. Head-spinning and steaming ears were not out of the question when Donald first learned of the incident. This would become the day that our son would learn his first sample of foul language. Actually, he learned several expletives that day and in the days that followed. Fortunately, before Brennan was totally versed in the world of profanity, Donald decided to get the model number off the lawnmower and buy a new set of keys from the dealer. Those lost keys would not be found for another year, when God chose to reveal them during a winter that left the tall grass frozen, short and dead.

Brennan and I developed a very special bond. I was certain that no parent had ever loved their child more and was even more certain that God had waited those six years to bless me with a son for a reason. Our bond would grow strong and I would rely on Brennan more than I would ever realize. I cherished my time with Brennan. We spent all of our time together, laughing and playing. Brennan had an amazing smile and a contagious laugh that got us through many dirty diapers and projectile cleanups together. Brennan provided us with a ton of entertainment as a toddler. He named his pacifier "uh-oh", because it fell out of his mouth so often. One summer day he came to me with the flyswatter and said, "Mom, there's a dammit fly in your room." I'm certain the tractor key incident had something to do with this.

I was a stay at home mother at this point and, as the books told me, would get together with friends and let our children play. These play dates affirmed for me what I already believed; that my child was the smartest, the cutest and most amazing child I had ever seen. I even entered him in a baby contest. I was uneasy about the entire process and questioned if this was the right thing for Brennan. I should have listened to my inner voice. It was total chaos. Hours passed as we waited for the "professionals" to get a look at my baby boy, who was by far the cutest baby in the competition; maybe the state . . . the world perhaps. He didn't win, didn't place, didn't even get a lousy pack of diapers, and in the end, I was, to say the least, defeated. This would be our last baby contest. I thanked God for the experience and promised that I would listen to that inner voice more closely next time.

A common theme began to emerge with people who saw Brennan for the first time, including the judges from the contest. Comments such as, "He is so little" were echoed far too often. I gave it very little consideration at first but the ever present comments were hard to ignore. Maybe I was in denial but it just didn't equate. Everyone at the hospital said he was the largest baby in the nursery, bigger than all the other babies. I immediately assumed I had done something wrong such as feeding him the wrong things. After the denial phase, came reluctant acceptance. Of course, I didn't have to look far to see where Brennan's genetic tree had fallen short—Donald and I weren't exactly redwoods. One by one, the other children his age were outgrowing him. My closest friends and I were pregnant at the same time, gave birth, had play dates and watched as each of their children outgrew Brennan. We asked about his growth at every doctor's visit, and at every visit we received the same answer, he was growing slowly, on his own curve. The doctor would show me growth charts where Brennan was and although he wasn't in the fiftieth percentile for height, he wasn't below the tenth percentile either. It was frustrating to hear my friends compare their gigantic children to mine. Some of my friends were kind enough to try to make me feel better. Other friends were blunt and would just come out and say things about his small size. His measurements on the growth chart were not enough to send him to a specialist, although we self-referred to one anyway. When Brennan was four, we took him to see an Endocrinologist. At the time, the doctor measured and weighed him and said the same thing as our regular doctor. He wasn't below the fifth percentile and so, there wasn't anything he could do for him. The doctors would often go to the obvious point and discuss Donald's and my stature, and explain that Brennan was just going to be small. This explanation would do for awhile but not forever.

Years later, as Brennan was entering the sixth grade we took him again to an endocrinologist. This time, they would do X-rays and blood tests along with measuring and weighing him. Brennan was diagnosed with Hashimoto's Thyroid disorder, an autoimmune disease in which the thyroid gland is gradually destroyed, leaving the patient with a number of possible results such as growth disruption. The disorder would impede his bone growth by as much as three years. Physically, he would always remain three years behind his peers. He would hit puberty, have normal growth spurts but each would be delayed by three years. He was placed on thyroid medicine and would have his growth monitored for the next several years. The doctors assured us that he would grow and that growth hormones would do nothing for him. We left there that day, knowing that he clearly had the same condition that his daddy had growing up. Donald knew how hard it was to not hit your growth spurt until after you graduated from high school. He wanted to help Brennan, but he didn't know how. No amount of attempted comfort helped. I tried saying things like, "Look on the bright side, you won't have acne and smell bad like those other boys"—nothing worked. Still, we hoped that he would hit a growth spurt and be able to play football like his daddy did. This had been Brennan's dream since he was old enough to hold a football. But Brennan's dreams, his daddy's dreams and my dreams for him would have to give way to God's plan. Letting go of that control was easier said than done, and looking back, it makes me sad to think that my dreams for him could have kept him from being everything that he should be, what he was born to be, what God meant for him to be.

> *So we fix our eyes not on what is seen, but on what is unseen. For what is seen is temporary, but what is unseen is eternal.—2 Corinthians 4:18*

The dreams that I had for Brennan were not unlike that of any parent who sees perfection in their child's reflection. Hopes and dreams that we have for our children are often dictated by society or peers. A parent has an idea of what their child will look like, act like. We have an idea of what kind of parents we will be, what our philosophy of parenting is. And then they arrive. They sleep, eat, cry, smile, snuggle and create unimaginable disasters in their diapers. All things we heard about, read about, were warned about but envisioned differently. The moment they are no longer in the womb, we think about them, we question ourselves and wonder if we are doing everything we can for them. We have this idea that everything will be normal, typical about them. They will be of average height and weight, will be of average, or above in athletic prowess and sociability. They will be money savvy and likeable. They will be responsible and make good decisions. They will test us, but eventually will see our reasoning and cave to our uncanny wisdom that comes with age and experience. Never into that picture does a parent envision being at the mercy of other children who are towering over our own. Never do we imagine worrying that our child might get hurt if he plays sports because he is so much smaller than others, even those much younger. Never do we imagine driving to doctor appointments instead of baseball games, or hospital stays in lieu of family vacations. My limited vision of the boy, who is average height, average weight, has perfect health and would lead his high school football team to multiple state championships was not at all what God had in mind. He saw a boy with an amazing sense of humor, a child who would draw the best out of everyone he encountered, a boy whose potential wasn't limited to 'ordinary', but who could easily be extraordinary. He saw the child who was compassionate and caring beyond his years. He saw the child who would bring cookies to church for his friends. God knew the boy, who as a preschooler, found out that one of his classmate's parents was in put in jail and came home, picked out one of his own toys and wrapped it up as a Christmas present for the child. My dreams for Brennan were insignificant, when compared to God's will. Brennan was a gift from God. I was just too focused on the wrapping. When I un-wrapped the gift, God allowed me to see so much more for Brennan than I could have ever imagined.

> *"The Lord does not look at the things man looks at. Man looks at the outward appearance, but the Lord looks at the heart." 1 Samuel 16:7*

CHAPTER 2

⇥❀⇤

When Brennan was almost three years old, God blessed us with another son, Adam Michael. Adam was born January 8, 2001. He was seven pounds, five ounces and a very smooth delivery. He was a beautiful boy and another favorite of the nursery staff. He was our second chance. No mistakes with this one. No mistakes . . . . but then again, it was just day one.

January 10th came and it was time to bring Adam home. Donald brought Brennan up to the hospital so we could go home as a family. Donald drove the car around as I sat in my wheelchair with my new baby boy, who apparently looked like me. I was happy that he looked like me because all I had heard about Brennan was that he looked like his daddy. As Donald walked to me from the car I saw a stressed, almost terrified, look on his face. He asked, "Do you have any keys to the car?" Under normal circumstances, this would have been a perfectly legitimate question. However, I had just spent the last couple of days in a postpartum hospital room and had no real answer to that, except for a shocked look with mouth open. "I locked the keys in the car! It's running and Brennan is locked in there," he said.

"Seriously?" I screamed. I could hardly move from childbirth, I desperately wanted to get home before this baby had to eat again and he locks our two year old in a running vehicle in the loading zone of the hospital. After about twenty minutes of trying to get the car-seat-bound two year old to press the unlock button on his door, we gave up. We called for a locksmith to open the door that would free our vehicle that would take us home. Never once did Brennan cry or seemed panicked. I can't say the same for Donald.

I was so sad for Brennan, I cried when I brought Adam home. It had just been Brennan and I for almost three years and I felt guilty for bringing this stranger into our home. Suddenly being a mother took on a new development, I was divided between two sons. Brennan was no longer my only focus. I had to focus on the baby too. I prayed to God to give me the strength and wisdom to share my love equally between both boys and to never let either feel the slightest bit neglected.

As a baby, Adam did not present the same challenges for me that his older brother did. He was very good at nursing and was an amazing sleeper, much to the delight of the entire family. I monitored Adam's growth closely and prayed that he would not have to battle with the same size issue as Brennan. I was relieved to see that Adam's growth was normal and could see that he would quickly outgrow his older brother. But Adam would have his own set of challenges.

Adam had middle ear problems, which is to say, he had ear infections repeatedly from birth well into his third year of life. At fifteen months, he had pressure equalizer tubes inserted and his adenoids removed to help alleviate his middle ear infections. By eighteen months, he had suffered through seven ear infections that had been treated by antibiotics. He always seemed to be congested, always had a runny nose, and always had fluid in his ears. I didn't realize how much this would affect his future. Adam was language delayed presumably from the ear infections, and so we sought help through the early intervention program in our state, Soonerstart. I knew a great deal about Soonerstart because I worked there as a Child Development Specialist for five years before I resigned to stay home with our first child, Brennan. I knew all about what it meant to be developmentally delayed enough to qualify for services through Soonerstart. To qualify, a child had to have at least two 25% delays or one 50% delay in an area of development. Adam had a 50% delay in language development. It took us more than six months to receive services due to the battle of who was going to serve us. Nobody in our county wanted to serve us because they were my friends, my colleagues; 'conflict of interest', they would call it. For six months, Adam would receive no assistance. Finally, another county gave us a resource coordinator and an entirely different county gave us a provider—a speech/language pathologist. For the first three months, I drove him thirty minutes to Tulsa to receive services. Once again, God provided a way.

Adam had both auditory processing and sensory integration problems. He was using sign language to communicate primarily. I had learned a few signs when I worked for Soonerstart, and taught him what I could. He knew the sign for "more", "milk", "eat", "drink", "book", "cat" and "bird". He used the sign for "more" most of the time. It got his needs met and we always used the verbal cue with it. We never used isolated signs. They were always paired with the spoken word. A child who isn't talking but is able to use sign language has less frustration when trying to communicate.

But Adam's array of health issues and medical concerns were not always natural. When he was twelve months old, Adam had his first MMR (measles, mumps and rubella) immunization. I was aware of the controversy that involved the MMR vaccine and autism and this was the immunization that worried me the most. Through Soonerstart, I had seen a child who, after having the MMR vaccine, stopped walking and talking and was having to be seen for speech and physical therapy. The MMR vaccine made me nervous.

At his fifteen month check-up, there was an apparent mistake with Adam's immunization record. His twelve month MMR vaccination had not been recorded so the doctor's office gave him another MMR vaccine. I was almost positive that he had already had one at his twelve month check-up, so I confronted the nurses at the office. They argued that if that was the case, it would be on his record. I gave in and baby Adam had his second MMR vaccine in three months, the same vaccine that I had seen completely incapacitate a one year old child years earlier. I consulted Adam's baby book and confirmed that he did have an MMR at twelve months. I contacted the doctor's office and they were apologetic. It wasn't enough for me. I contacted the local Health Department who indicated that he would be fine, as long as the injections were one month apart, the MMR vaccine he received at fifteen months would count as his second injection. At his two year check-up, when the nurses wanted to give him his second MMR shot, I was able to tell them that he had already had two when they messed up and gave him one at twelve months, and one at fifteen months. They let it go and we would be allowed to go home without much of a fight, but they had still not documented in his record that he had had two MMR shots, a fact that I was certain of and had charted in his baby book. I was diligent about his baby book and was very good at updating it and I knew that I was right about this. When Adam was three years old, we scheduled his three year check-up. I was unable to go so Donald took Adam to his appointment. We had so much going on at the time that it was impossible for either of us to know what was about to happen at his three year visit. Adam received yet another MMR vaccine. I was absolutely terrified. Adam, who was already speech delayed had his third MMR vaccine in two years. Of course, I was angry with my husband who had unknowingly allowed them to give him this shot. I had always been there at his doctor appointments, I had always protected him. I was sick to my stomach. I felt completely alone as the protector of my children; I could rely on nobody to do it as well as I could. It was just one of many times that I felt completely pulled in different directions, trying desperately to mother both of my children, and not being able to do it. I was again helpless to rewind time and go back to change what had happened, something I desperately wanted to do. I again, found myself, face down in my pillow crying and pleading with God to protect my son from the poison he had just been injected with. I prayed that God would not allow any harm to come to him because of my negligence and helplessness. I waited and watched as closely as I could to determine if there had been any ill effects from the vaccine. I noticed nothing and found that perhaps my prayers had again been answered. God protected my boy.

Prayer was my constant source of strength and I needed that strength more than ever. As the boys aged, their lives became busier and more complicated. Adam's ability to speak and understand the spoken word was not improving. Brennan was entering school and becoming more active. I looked to God daily for strength and guidance. We knew we had our hands full. Brennan was entering Kindergarten—half-day, and I was serving on the PTO at his school trying to be involved in his education while driving Adam to Tulsa for speech therapy and audiological evaluations trying to help him learn how to talk. With the fluid in his ear, Adam hadn't heard things correctly for the first eighteen months of his life. The neurons in his brain that should have been firing with sharpness and ease were not. This is what determines how successful we are with learning language. Those neurons were firing fuzzily, unsure, connections breaking down creating a speech disorder called Apraxia. He had problems saying sounds and words. He knew what he wanted to say, his brain just had problems moving the body parts needed for speech. Adam didn't know where his body was in space or his tongue was in his mouth, which was the primary problem. Automatic, reflexive movements such as breathing, sucking, swallowing were all good; learning to talk was not. But I kept things in perspective and thanked God for my beautiful boys.

As they aged, the boys quickly became unique and their differences were fun to watch evolve. Adam was a quirky little boy. He loved trains. Thomas the Train was his favorite. He would play for hours with his train track and trains. He would watch the movies and listen to the songs. I bought them originally for Brennan, but he didn't touch them. Brennan was much too interested in having and keeping my attention. Adam was obsessed with Thomas movies, toys, lunch boxes, flashlight, music, and everything in between; if it existed Adam owned it. Adam was very unique to say the least. He was always an adventurer, no matter what the weather was like outside. Extreme cold temperatures didn't seem to bother him. He would wander outside in the snow in nothing but a diaper and boots. He climbed everything. He mastered the ladder of the bunk bed at eleven months. I was amazed, and terrified, to walk in and see him fully standing in his diaper at the top of the bunk bed; but that was just Adam. Bunk beds weren't the only thing he could climb. He climbed cabinets, entertainment centers and I even found him on the top of my refrigerator. I was exasperated and concerned at the same time. I had no idea where to hide things such as knives and poisonous cleaner from a child who could seemingly scale the walls of any room in the house.

As the boys grew, another reoccurring side effect emerged. The play dates became fewer as parents who had one or two children who were "normal" knew inviting us over was likely much more work for them. A few of them, who remain as Angels today, stood by me through those crazy years. But most of the invitations stopped, especially once Adam could climb on any counter, and jump on and off any bed. The boys began to fight, not argue—fight. Mothers with boys would tell me—oh that is normal. At times they were unstoppable and not something I expected. I continued to pray for strength and continued to praise God for the two boys that I had been blessed with; the same two boys who were now fighting more often than not. The fighting frustrated me and often made me physically ill. At least I thought it was the fighting.

> *And we urge you, brothers, warn those who are idle, encourage the timid, help the weak, be patient with everyone. 1 Thessalonians 5:14*

CHAPTER 3

A few months after Adam turned two, I learned I was pregnant again. God's plan for this pregnancy was a mystery to me because we had tried for so long to get pregnant with both boys and yet this time there was no planning at all. Things were different, immediately. I was sick, both mentally and physically. This baby was making me very sick. Barely able to eat anything I was sick, exhausted and was sleeping all the time. I couldn't seem to keep up with the two I had on the ground and I had another one coming. I went through phases of anger, doubt and insecurities. Why would God think I was ready for another one? I was barely able to take care of the two I was trying to raise; one who was extremely small for his age and the other wasn't talking and had been diagnosed with Apraxia. I was not ready for this!

We had all the tests run that pregnant women over 35 have done. The triple screen came back suspect. They called me on New Year's Eve 2003 with less than good news. The result from the triple screen was low for protein, an indication of Down's syndrome. An ultrasound was ordered for verification. I was an emotional wreck—how could this be happening? I spent the next several nights praying that God would not give me more than I could handle, that He would give me strength to deal with whatever was going on with this baby.

One week later, we were in the ultrasound room. The attending nurse paused as she watched the screen. She stood and excused herself to get the doctor. She didn't need to do or say anything else to confirm what I already knew—**twins**. I said "There are two aren't there?"

She said "Yes." My husband fell to his knees and they had to go get another nurse for him. I began to cry because I knew what that meant, or at least I thought I knew. My sister had twins six years ago and she was just now starting to look like a normal person. She was an exhausted, brain-dead nightmare for the first year after they were born and gradually came out of her shock a little more with each year of their growth. I watched her cry many times. I helped her buy diapers, and formula, I would baby sit whenever I could and I prayed many prayers for her strength. All that of course, before I had my own little gems that I loved more than life but were taking more than their share of my sanity.

Donald finally sat up as the doctor came in to verify that there were two. Of course I unleashed my frustration on the doctor. I had told him before that I thought there were two but he always insisted there was only one heartbeat. It was a small victory for my pride that would be short lived. "We don't see a membrane," the ultrasound tech declared. When I asked what that meant, I was told that it meant I had to see a specialist, a Perinatologist. Twin B was smaller than twin A, much smaller. The doctors were worried. I was too ignorant to be worried; I was panicked, I was angry and I felt alone. After leaving the doctor's office, I went straight home to my boys and I hugged them. I felt extremely guilty that I was bringing complete and total chaos into their home, not that it wasn't already a little chaotic. But life was about to be thrust into the world of the four ring circus featuring different attractions, none of which you could watch fully without being distracted by the other.

I was on the verge of a meltdown with all of this new information, new terms and new fears. I was scared, angry and convinced that I was about to embark on a journey that would test my strength and my faith. I prayed repeatedly and yet repeatedly my mind went to the terms being used by the doctors and specialists. But instead of dwelling in sadness and confusion, I chose to arm myself with education.

I began doing Internet research on twins with no membrane. The results were not exactly favorable with most experts agreeing on a fifty percent mortality rate. The twins could end up being so big around the sixth month that they become in danger of strangling themselves or each other with the umbilical cords. The mothers typically have to be on bed rest for the last three months of the pregnancy. Bed rest was a not an option; not for me. The more I read, the more I began to panic. Tearfully, I prayed like I hadn't prayed up to that point before. I began to beg God for help:

> "Please God, help the specialist to find a membrane, there has to be a membrane. God, you know I can't be on bed rest for three months. My boys will kill each other—not to mention what my husband will think."

The following day, I met with the Perinatologist. Sitting on the bed, I noticed a table with a needle that was easily eight inches long, sterile pads and a syringe. I was praying that those were not for me. She did the ultrasound and spoke the words I had been begging God to hear, "There is a membrane, look you can see it right here." She showed it to me, I could see it. It seemed to be cradling, outlining Twin B, my tiny baby. I was elated. But once again, a victory that proved to be short lived. Twin A was all over the place; the space was huge and so was Twin A in comparison to Twin B. My happiness at the membrane was suddenly stifled by her next set of words. "You have a condition called TTTS, Twin-to-Twin Transfusion Syndrome." My heart sank, although what she said made very little sense. I thought "membrane" meant healthy babies, no bed rest, happiness, or at least some semblance of order.

"There is no cure," she said. "Your babies share a placenta. They also share blood vessels within the placenta. Currently Twin A is receiving the majority of the blood and food that your placenta is giving to the babies. Twin B, is receiving little, if any. The treatment is the removal of amniotic fluid from Twin A's sac, this is a temporary fix. It allows Twin B some room to move and grow. But by next week, possibly a matter of days, it will look like this again and will require another treatment which will again remove the excess fluid from Baby A's sac. You will not take home one baby from this, you will have two or you will have none. They have less than a twenty percent chance of surviving but they will be early regardless. Prematurity carries its own set of problems with it, but if they survive the Twin-to-Twin Transfusion Syndrome, they will be born prematurely." My heart sank, I started to cry uncontrollably. Thank God, my mother was there with some words of comfort and encouragement. And thankfully God was and is there, always.

The next few days were pure torture. I was a complete and total mess. I didn't understand why God would be putting me through this. I prayed again and again. There were so many questions, so many doubts. Finally at my lowest point, I felt a pull on my heart. Something changed within me. Suddenly I felt it—I had to have these babies. I felt the renewed mother bear inside of me rear up. I knew the chances of them surviving were slim but I would fight with every ounce of my being to get them here. I would pray with every fiber to ask God to let me have them, if only for a little while, to hold them, name them.

In my distress I called to the LORD; I cried to my God for help. From his temple he heard my voice; my cry came before him, into his ears. Psalm 18:6

I knew the chances were very slim that I would give birth to the twins. My prayers became more frequent and more focused. I thanked God for blessing me with the boys I had and prayed that He would allow me to hold the twins and watch them breathe their first breaths of air. I prayed for the doctors, for the specialists and nurses. I knew that the coming days were going to be very difficult and very trying for all of us. But from somewhere deep inside, I now had a renewed faith and a determination to have these babies.

I was seventeen weeks along and I knew this visit would require every prayer for strength and courage that I could think of. This time that eight inch needle on the table would be for me. The specialist began the procedure of my first amnioreduction. During this procedure, I would lie on my back and she would insert that eight inch needle into my stomach using the ultrasound as a guide in order to avoid hitting either baby with the needle. She would extract as much amniotic fluid out of my babies' womb as possible until the risk was too great of hitting Twin A. With each reduction procedure, the chance of losing both twins was enormous. At any point, infection could be introduced. She could hit either one or both of the babies with the needle. The needle could irreparably puncture the membrane so that it would be unable to heal itself and continue to leak without remedy, killing both twins.

The drive home that day was almost unbearable. Once there the ability to stay positive, which was essential, was my most difficult task. Again, my coping mechanism of knowledge-seeking took over and I found myself on the Internet trying to find out everything I could about twin-to-twin transfusion syndrome. I found one site that was a memorial to all of the babies that had been lost due to this syndrome. This made me sad, scared and sick. Very few survived and of those who did, most were diagnosed with cerebral palsy caused from brain bleeds that were due to being born too early. I was desperate. I called my sister and we had our biggest heart to heart talk that we have ever had in our lives.

I was convinced that God was trying to teach me something. I was raised to believe that each struggle I encountered in this world was devised to teach me something; something that would bring me closer to God. I feared that the lesson I needed to learn was that of loss, a lesson that would teach me to appreciate my boys, the children who were alive. God knew that I loved my boys. He also knew they were driving me crazy with their aggression and anger towards each other. The fighting, I had hated the fighting. But I longed for that now. I longed to be able to see my twins survive, fight, argue and live. I did not want to be the mom that buried her babies; the mom that people would see in the supermarket and not know what to say. I told my sister that I firmly believed the lesson God was trying to teach me was one of loss. She told me that she believed it was possible for God to change His mind. That thought hadn't occurred to me. Had the prayers of His people ever changed God's plan? I did the first thing anyone would do with such a question—I called my mother. My mother had taught Sunday school for years. She and my dad would debate the teachings of the Bible for hours in the night. I asked her, "Had God ever changed His mind at the request, the pleas of His people?" She said He had and I was renewed with hope. I was still eighty percent despair and twenty percent hope. But it was more than I had left the doctor's office with. I began to pray, not just the "Hey God, oh by the way" prayer but the pleading, bawling, begging prayer of a mother who was desperate to have her babies born alive. I told Him that I understood if I needed a lesson on loss in order to better appreciate my children. But I pleaded with Him to teach me in another way:

> "God please. I know how hard it is to raise twins, so in essence, allowing them to live would teach me many lessons. Dear Lord Jesus, please let me know my babies, please let me have a chance to hold them and kiss them, even if it is only for a few years. I will savor every minute of their lives for as long as You will allow me to call them mine, until You take them for Your own. But not yet, Lord, let me have them for a little while, I beg."

This is the confidence we have in approaching God: that if we ask anything according to His will, he hears us.—1 John 5:14

Every week I would go to the specialist literally shaking, trembling that this might be the day that she would find no heartbeat in one or both. I would wake up every morning and wait, wait to feel something, anything. Once I felt it, I would rise and shower and begin my day, hopeful that they were still alive, for now. I was determined to document their life for as little as they were in my womb. Ultrasounds every week, measurements and still pictures ensured that they would be easily documented in a "My Pregnancy" book. The doctor would place the ultrasound wand on my belly—one heartbeat, two heartbeats. She measured the bladders of the babies, which showed how much kidney function they had. Twin A always had a huge bladder. Twin B rarely, if ever, had even a discernible bladder. Kidney failure for Twin B was always a fear, as was stroke. Heart attack for Twin A was the most likely because the heart would be unable to process all the blood flow and food given to it from the placenta.

I was always thankful to hear that the twins were still alive and that there was still hope. Most of the weekly appointments didn't offer much more than that. Encouragement was slim but with each week, I hung on to the hopes that God was giving me. I continued to pray and continued to thank God for the blessings I had. But eventually the news would change.

Finally, I was blessed with an appointment that showed some real positive news. They sent some amniotic fluid off for a karyotype. The results showed completely healthy identical **baby girls**; healthy, except for the ever dooming twin-to-twin transfusion syndrome. This announcement made my prayers and my resolve ever more diligent. I was more determined than ever to fight hard for my baby girls; two baby girls that were fighting every moment to stay alive. Again, the doctor prepared the needle for another amnioreduction. Those made me sick to my stomach; faint almost. They would position a fan in front of me because I would sweat so much. I also could not lie completely flat so they had to keep me propped up so I didn't pass out. I focused completely on the song "I Can Only Imagine" throughout my amnioreductions. The needle placed in my stomach was positioned and repositioned to make the most out of the reductions. Too many reductions and the membrane would collapse, too little and Twin B would starve to death and have a stroke, which would cause Twin A to have a heart attack. "You will not leave with one baby, you will have two or none," echoed in my mind time and again. After about twenty minutes, the needle would be removed and a band-aid placed over the puncture wound. I was left to go home and hope that they would still be alive next week for our appointment. I would read "Extreme TTTS" at the bottom of my pink sheet as I took it to the receptionist to check out. Everything seemed to be extreme at this point. My faith was strong, my fears were real; it was a difficult balance to maintain. It was all or nothing and I knew my hopes and prayers were to see my girls. I just prayed that God's plan might be the same.

> *"For I know the plans I have for you," declares the LORD, "plans to prosper you and not to harm you, plans to give you hope and a future." Jeremiah 29:11*

CHAPTER 4

✦❀✦

Brennan was five now and Adam was three. Adam had begun putting more words together but he was still very difficult to understand. At three, the school system was responsible for giving Adam speech therapy and so we went once or twice a week for thirty minute therapy sessions with the school therapist. Brennan was learning to read in kindergarten and I was so very proud of him. Brennan loved school and was progressing nicely through my mental checklist. Adam had not quite mastered toilet training. He had no interest in it. He was happy as ever just to use his diaper. I was having the difficulty. It was very hard to change a diaper while being pregnant with twins and Adam's legs were almost as long as mine. Adam was growing quickly; at three, he was almost as tall as his five year old brother. This was a fact that Brennan was not very happy about. Ironically, people would ask if the boys were twins. People would also ask when I was due and if the "baby" was a boy or a girl. I would say, "THEY are due in June, but will likely come in April. I am having twins."

"Oh twins," they would say, "how wonderful. You will have your hands full."

Each time I would smile and say, "I hope so."

I was advised by doctors and specialists to have cautious optimism. I was even advised to not purchase baby books or baby clothes until the twins were in their 27th week. The 27th week would be a good indication of survival, although they were viable at 24 weeks. The weekly amnioreductions would continue, although some were not as scheduled as others. Sometimes, I would get a funny feeling and I would call the doctor and say, "I think something is wrong." It was at those times, I ended up needing two reductions in one week. Most were uneventful but week twenty saw a transition. One of our greatest fears of the amnioreductions occurred. The specialist inadvertently poked a hole in Twin B's membrane while extracting fluid from Twin A's sac. It was easily seen in the ultrasound. What could have been a disaster, God turned into a blessing. Suddenly, Twin B had fluid surrounding her, she wasn't as stuck and she had fluid in her bladder. It was the most exhilarating visit up to this point. The doctor actually turned to me with a smile on her face. This was something I had not really seen to date, she was always so serious. She admitted to me on that day, she was certain I was going to lose those babies, but today—she said, she felt hopeful. She decided to put me on full bed rest. I could get up to shower every other day, other than that—I was instructed to lay on my right side and drink protein shakes in addition to eating well. I was to do this until I delivered or lost the babies, whichever came first. Once again, a small victory that was short lived.

The week after our hopeful news, everything was back to the way it was. The accidental hole in Twin B's membrane had closed and she was again without any fluid in her sac. Hope dwindled but we decided it was time to name the babies. Tiny Twin B would be Emma, and the larger Twin A would be Allison, Allie for short. It is a tough day, naming children who I might have to bury. In my darkest hours, my mind drifted to what their tombstones would look like, what we would sing at their funeral, what flowers would be there. Part of me couldn't let myself imagine them actually getting here. I explained to Brennan what was going on, why his mother was confined to the couch during the day and her bed at night. I told him that Allie was swimming in a big pool of water, while Emma had only a puddle. I told him that he needed to pray for his sisters, that they might not make it. He understood completely, as much as a five-year old first born son can, and commenced to praying that very evening before bed.

Initially, I had said the order of bed rest was simply not an option. I led an active life trying to keep up with the boys and their active lives. It had been a long, tough winter but spring and warmer temperatures were on the way. But for me, enjoying warm spring days would have to give way to bed rest and a test of patience. Not being able to get my child more chocolate milk, do my own shopping, pay bills, keep up with laundry, cooking, cleaning; it was rough. It was during this time that God first showed me what kind of support system I had in place. My dad would do the shopping, my mom paid bills for me, did laundry, fed the children during the day. My friends had put together meals for me, every other day in the evenings. I had friends taking Brennan and Adam to school, and friends picking them up and bringing them home to me. I had friends loaning me books to read and movies to watch. I talked on the phone for hours to help deal with the boredom. My mom and dad would drive me to my appointments, they were amazingly supportive. Whenever I would feel badly about requiring so much help, mom would say, "God is blessing these people; don't rob them of their blessings." It was easier then, but I hoped with all of my heart that someday I could re-pay them.

Week 24—the specialist decided to do the amnioreductions at the hospital, because the babies were viable at 24 weeks and if something went wrong they could be taken to the NICU quickly.

Week 27—the specialist announced that I was to be taken to the hospital immediately where I would remain throughout the remainder of the pregnancy.

I called my husband, who was already at his wit's end, and told him. I was crying because I knew we were at a point where I had to relinquish all control of what happened at home. My parents drove me to the hospital where the staff was waiting for me. I gave my mother a list of things that I wanted from home that would make me feel better. Pictures of the boys, chocolate mini-eggs, and finally the girls' baby books. I needed to get started on those, and I knew I was going to have the time. The week days weren't horrible. I had an amazingly kind and loving nurse who always greeted me with a smile. She did share that she had seen a couple other pregnancies with TTTS but none that had survived. She said when they were born, one was always very small and pale while the other was bigger and blood red. That made sense. I was pretty matter-of-fact about it. I believed at this point that God had

23

possibly changed His mind and that He was going to let me get to know these babies. I believed beyond a doubt however, that other lessons were sure to follow, that He hadn't changed His mind about what He wanted me to learn, but rather the way in which He was choosing to teach me.

> *Trust in the LORD with all your heart; and lean not upon your own understanding. In all your ways acknowledge him, and he shall direct your path. Proverbs 3:5-6*

The boys would come up and visit, mostly they focused on pushing the buttons on the bed and seeing how many times they could flush the toilet in my room. Donald could usually make it 30 minutes and then it was time for them to go. I didn't like watching them go. It made me sad and homesick. Plus, I was huge—at least I felt huge, and stretched to the limit. After they removed fluid, I always felt better for about a day or so, then the tightness, uncomfortable feeling would come back. I had heartburn, not your normal everyday heartburn where you pop a couple of antacids and go on your way. I had heartburn so bad that I couldn't lay back or drink water. It was the worst heartburn I could possibly imagine. But I thanked God each day for that heartburn, thankful that the girls were growing big enough to cause me such heartburn.

I had my final amnioreduction, one for the record books at the hospital. They removed five pounds of fluid. Five pounds was more than both of the babies weighed together. The specialist was able to measure them and give an estimate as to how much they weighed. At 29 weeks, Emma weighed 1 pound 15 ounces, and Allie weighed 2 pounds 14 ounces. The doctors were worried about Emma. She wasn't quite two pounds which can increase complications in prematurity. She was at higher risk for brain bleeds which could cause her to have neurological problems for the rest of her life. I prayed but knew at this point, it was out of my hands.

The morning of the 14th of April, my water started to leak. I searched around frantically looking for some paper, the special paper you can wipe with to see if it is amniotic fluid or urine, a trick I had learned in the hospital when I was in labor with the boys. I couldn't find any of that magic paper so called the nurse. At 5:00 a.m., the nurse came in with the magic paper and told me it was indeed amniotic fluid I was leaking. They were contacting the doctors. I called my parents and my husband. I couldn't reach Donald, no one was answering in the shop where he worked. I tried two more times and left a message, assuming he would come when he got it. I was being prepped for an emergency C-section. They were preparing and scuttling busily around me. Every now and then I would cry, and my precious nurse would assure me that everything would be okay. I told her to promise me that she would take a picture of them before they stuck any of the tubes on them. She promised, and I gave her my camera.

I had two vaginal births prior to this, one which required stitches. The C-section was much worse. I was on my back, dry heaving into an empty bucket. I could hear a song playing in the background . . . "The first Cut is the Deepest . . ." I was unable to breathe. I saw very quickly one baby out, then the second, and then I was out. My blood pressure plummeted, my heart rate dropped; I was dying. More than once, medical equipment monitoring my vital statistics indicated that I had died on the table. Attention quickly moved from the twins to saving me. Through God's grace, I awoke to a room full of family and friends all looking at me. My questions immediately were about the girls. They said the girls were in the NICU and they were being worked on. They were 1 pound 15 ounces and 2 pounds 14 ounces, exactly. Beside me were two pictures that were taken of the girl's right after they were born. Emma looked very small, uncooked almost and very pale. Allie was bigger, still uncooked looking but very red. I felt awful, I was sick from the anesthesia and for the first time in my life had given birth, but had no baby to show for it. They were gone, not far, but they were not with me, and wouldn't be for another eight weeks. God had blessed me by giving them to me for now, but I could hardly wait to see them, touch them.

Throughout the many weeks of pregnancy with the twins, I had prayed to God and saw His hands at work in many ways. The support and love of my friends and family during a time when uncertainty was a constant, the inadvertent puncture of Emma's membrane which may have actually allowed her to develop more and the amazing talents of the medical support staff who cared for not only my babies, but saved my life on the table. But shortly after delivery, I received another sign of just how blessed I had been and just how powerful prayer is.

> *But certainly God has heard me; He has given heed to the voice of my prayer. Psalm 66:19*

I had a total of thirteen amnioreductions, which were not pleasant. My specialist came in not long after I had given birth and told me that the membrane usually fails after five amnioreductions. No one had ever been able to sustain a membrane for thirteen amnioreductions, it was unheard of. I knew who held that membrane together, my Lord Jesus. God had changed His mind, and although unpleasant and difficult at the time, I was going to know, love and hold those baby girls. It was everything I had prayed for.

> *Cast your cares on the Lord and he will sustain you; he will never let the righteous fall.—Psalm 55:22*

CHAPTER 5

→❀←

That night, three of my friends brought me dinner and watched a movie with me. I know they saved me that night from the loneliness I was certain to feel. The movie was a comedy and it hurt to laugh. I had been cut from one side to another on my abdomen and I was in a lot of pain. But I loved that they were there. It would have been tough to be there alone, and with no babies. The nurses wheeled in my electric breast pump which I was to start using immediately. The babies needed to eat, through a tube, but they needed my milk. It was something, something I could do for them, so far away. So I pumped, every two hours and through the night. The next day brought new visitors. Each bringing support and kind words of encouragement. I was still not well enough to leave my room. I wanted desperately to make the trek to the NICU to look at my girls. I wanted to see for myself that they were okay. The NICU was a rollercoaster ride; the doctors and nurses kept saying, "One step forward, two steps back." It was difficult because other people could go see my babies—but not me, not yet. My body was healing but my spirit was sinking fast.

Day three of postpartum, a nurse came in and said, "If you feel up to it, we will take you down to see your girls." Another answered prayer. I had to pick a time when my nurse was available and between pumping times. Finally, they wheeled me down the hallway to the NICU. I stood painfully to wash my hands, a practice they took very seriously. I sat back down in my wheelchair and they wheeled me in to see Allie. She was tiny, so tiny I couldn't believe she was alive. I started to cry. I hated that she was hooked up to all of those machines, that I had to make a trip down the hall just to see her, that I couldn't hold her, and worst of all—that she was across the NICU from her sister. I kept saying "She is so tiny, I can't believe how tiny she is."

A nurse heard me and said, "Well if you think she is tiny, you better not go look at your other baby." I immediately asked to see her. They wheeled me over to Emma and sure enough, she was very small, unbelievably small, like a tiny doll. She had even more tubes in her and she was under the bilirubin lights—purple lights that made her skin look almost snakelike, mottled red and white splotches. Then the highlight; they asked me if I wanted to hold Allie. I was ecstatic, holding her and Emma were all I had hoped for, all I had prayed for since this nightmare pregnancy began. They let me hold her, but no more than five minutes at a time. They set a timer and promptly placed her back in her bed when the time was up. I didn't realize how much pain I was in until they removed her from my arms; too much too soon. But I was happy that I had gotten to meet them and I felt God's presence so fully. I was happy to call them my girls; my genetically perfect, identical twins who just happened to be very tiny and fragile. I went back to my room and pumped again. What struck me most about the NICU, even though they were lifesavers, where my girls were concerned, was a specific feeling; the feeling that they weren't quite mine. I was allowed to remove a baby from her box, but only with permission. I could hold that baby for a limited period of time, but only with the constant eye of trained professionals. And, when instructed, I was to put the baby back into her box and leave the unit. I resented them for that. I had fought tooth and nail and had prayed for almost eight months for these babies. One of the older nurses asked me if these were my first. I said, "No, I have two boys. One is six and the other is three."

She asked, "Do they listen to you?"

"No," I said.

She followed with, "Well, I didn't say this but what you need is a yard stick, that way you can hold and feed the babies, while whacking them boys when they don't listen." I actually had a yardstick at home, it was a thought.

I was allowed to go home on day four. It was difficult and painful, physically and emotionally, to leave the hospital without my babies. This was something I had never done before and the feeling left me empty and sad. But this was quickly remedied by the reunion with my boys. I missed my boys badly. I was excited to get to see them again. It had been almost a month. I came home to two boys who, for all intents and purposes were not going to let me out of their sight. I was still pumping every two hours and through the night. Donald and I were taking turns visiting the girls. He would go up one day and I the next. We were only able to stay an hour or two. The NICU was mandatorily vacated during shift change, and the girls could only handle so much stimulation. The boys, especially Brennan, were constantly asking when they could go see their sisters. No one under twelve was allowed in the NICU, ever. Rules were rules, but we did decide to bring them up and hold the girls up to the window, so they could see. Brennan would cry. He was devastated that he couldn't go in and hold and see his sisters; the sisters that he had prayed for every night and already felt a deep connection with. It was difficult, leaving the boys to go see the girls, and then leaving the girls to go see the boys. Many tears were shed on those drives; many prayers for guidance and strength, but mostly prayers of thanks and appreciation.

Allie recovered quickly. She had a few problems with her heart and her kidneys, residual from being the 'recipient' twin and having to process too much blood and food from the placenta. Emma, the donor twin, was doing amazingly well for what doctors termed an Extremely Low Birth Weight baby and Small for Gestational Age. Neither of them had to be on a vent. They were on the C-Pap machine but only for 24 hours. Their MRI's had shown no brain bleeds, which was perhaps the best news of all. We were just waiting for them to grow. They would have to grow and learn how to suck, swallow and breathe so that they could eat from a bottle. They would also have to pass a sleep study, fit in a car seat and their daddy and I would have to take and pass CPR and a couple of other preparatory classes before we would be able to take them home.

Week seven arrived and we were allowed to take Allie home. She would have to remain on an apnea monitor 24 hours a day. It was bittersweet for me, taking Allie home, but leaving Emma at the hospital. Three days later, we brought Emma home. It was the start of something that we could never have imagined. The start of something amazing and chaotic, a blessing and a hardship—apnea monitors.

Little did we know that something so small would cause us to get absolutely no sleep. The apnea monitor is geared to wake up anyone within a 500 foot radius. It not only goes off when the baby stops breathing for more than thirty seconds, but it also goes off if there is a loose lead that is supposed to be connected to the baby. So, I was awake feeding Emma every two hours, pumping when I was not feeding and resetting the apnea monitors that went off throughout the night due to a "loose lead". Throughout my life, sleep had always been a most precious thing, and without it, my moods are unpredictable. I would always feed Emma while Donald always fed Allie. Allie would sleep longer and take five minutes to take her entire bottle. Emma was not that cooperative. Emma would wake every two hours and take twenty minutes to finish a bottle. Emma also had a tendency to not keep her milk down long. More times than not she would projectile vomit the entire feeding and I would have to start all over again. The least little thing would upset Emma to the point that she would projectile vomit an entire feeding. Often times Donald would feed Allie and would turn the TV on, sound muted. Just the television light was enough to over-stimulate Emma to the point that she would projectile vomit an entire meal. It was not pretty.

A week in to what we refer to as "the time we don't speak about", Allie's monitor was going off every ten minutes. At first, I thought it was a loose lead. About half way through her record of fifty apnea episodes in one night, I leaned over her, quietly, steadily and listened to her. I listened to her breathing. I listened to her stop breathing and I began to count to thirty, when her monitor would go off. Sometimes, she would continue to stop breathing for up to forty-five seconds. That was as long as I could wait and I had to shake her into breathing again. Immediately that morning, I called the doctor. He was extremely worried and asked us to bring her back to the Neonatal Intensive Care Unit, the NICU.

We drove her in, defeated and exhausted. Something was very wrong, but we didn't know what. She had been doing so well. I passed her off to the doctor reluctantly. She was screaming and I was sick to my stomach. How could I leave her here again? What is going on? Why was she so sick? What does she have? These questions would go unanswered, as every test they ran came back normal. They released her back to us four days later. We took her home without answers, but she seemed better. Her monitor wasn't going off as often and we were getting some sleep. The evenings were the most difficult. Donald worked evenings, left the house at 2:30 in the afternoon and did not get home until 11:00 or so at night. If he stopped after work to workout at the gym, it would be closer to 12:30 a.m. when he would be home to help me. Of course, the boys would come home from school and would deteriorate until what I called the "six o'clock hour". The "six o'clock hour" was a time when the children were hungry, tired and grumpy from their day. I was still pumping breast milk every two to three hours, the girls were still eating every two to three hours and they were still on apnea monitors. I couldn't hold them both at the same time because they got irritated if they touched or kicked each other, so I held them one at a time. Bouncy seats were a lifesaver. I could put the girls in their bouncy seats and feed them their bottles and pump at the same time. I didn't do it often, but I could do it if I had to. There were days when I literally didn't eat for hours. I would forget to eat, bathe, brush my teeth, and brush my hair. I was in mother mode. I was mothering all day. I was groped, smothered, fought over, sleep-deprived, and stressed. On the nights the girls were screaming and the boys were fighting and I was about to pass out from not eating, I would call my mom and dad. They would rush right over and hold a baby, which is just what I needed. They were precious, caring grandparents who would hold the babies while I ate, while I snuggled the boys, while I did the dishes, laundry, bathed, brushed my teeth, brushed my hair, anything else. It was an answer to prayer. My parents lived close. They were only a phone call away. Thankfully, they always seemed to sense the desperation in my voice and they rushed right over. Sometimes, they would stay for hours until I got the boys to bed, and they knew the crisis was over. One night, I was on the couch pumping and Adam was on the couch. He had caught some type of stomach bug. Brennan was on the toilet and was yelling "I'm done"—code for come wipe my bottom. The girls were on the floor on a blanket, screaming their heads off. I looked at Adam just as he vomited all over the fabric couch. With all of the chaos, I ripped the pump off of me and began to put Adam in the bathtub to clean him up. I wiped Brennan's bottom and continued to bathe Adam, who was only three years old. The girls were still screaming on the floor and the pump was still going in the living room. I came back out and started to clean up the couch. It was useless and I was on the brink of a nervous breakdown. I called my mom and dad and they rushed right over. It was the end of my pumping; I just could not do it anymore. I couldn't sit for twenty minutes every two hours without the prospect of an interruption; it was impossible. I had enough breast milk frozen to get the girls through their first seven months of life. But after it was gone, I decided I would be buying formula for the two babies.

We couldn't take the girls places. We definitely couldn't take them places where there were many people, or other children. They were at risk for all kinds of diseases, the least of which was RSV—respiratory syncytial virus. Although RSV is very common with children, the hospital told us it could be fatal to the girls. They were both still hooked up to apnea monitors, which made it extremely difficult to haul them anywhere. So we mostly went to the doctor appointments, church, and home. There was no way we could do movies, zoos or even restaurants. We even had a professional photographer come to the house to take pictures of them. Everyone who loved us and loved them wanted to see them, hold them, and meet them; they were the miracle babies. They were an answer to prayers, many people's prayers, not just mine. I felt selfish not taking them to Christmas parties and family reunions.

We were immediately referred to Soonerstart from the hospital. The twins were developmentally delayed. They were ten weeks early, so at nearly three months, they were like newborns. And so began the days of speech, occupational and physical therapy for the girls. It was good for them. They did well and tolerated the therapy well. For them, it was play-time. It was hard on the boys when the attention was focused so much on the girls.

In August of 2004, the twins were about four months old and I was contacted by the Neonatologist. He recommended that both twins be removed from the apnea monitors. We were cautiously optimistic but unsure. Since bringing the twins home, we had relied on the monitors to alert us if either twin stopped breathing. Sleepless nights aside, the monitors had been the only way of knowing that the twins were breathing. It was time to trust that God would keep the twins safe and keep their breathing regular. The advantages were immediate as it became much easier to transport the girls and sleep became a more regular part of our night. It was a good transition, one of many that we would go through as the girls got older. Once again, our trust in God and prayers were rewarded.

> *Do not fear, for I am with you; do not anxiously look about you, for I am your God. I will strengthen you, surely I will help you, surely I will uphold you with My righteous right hand—Isaiah 41:10*

CHAPTER 6

⟿❈⟾

As the girls grew and developed, I began to notice differences in their behaviors. Throughout the pregnancy, doctors were most concerned about Twin B, Emma, and her survival chances. As was expected she was the smallest, weakest and most likely to show symptoms of the Twin-to-Twin Transfusion Syndrome. Also to be expected, she remained in the hospital days after Twin A, Allie, was released to go home to her family. However, in a bizarre twist it was Allie who appeared to be the one that showed more signs of prematurity and over-stimulation. Episodes of screaming and flailing arms and legs were long lasting and far too common.

I remember vividly the times when the 'prematurity' and the 'overstimulation' would kick in. I recorded the two hour long screaming, flailing fits Allie would have. It was like suddenly, she was in agony. I couldn't console her. She wanted me, but she didn't want me. I would videotape her because I had never heard of this type of behavior in my life. I had read the books, they all instructed to ignore it, or walk away. So I did. She would roll and flail and scream towards me. After an hour, I just couldn't take it so I would lock myself in my bathroom and call for help. Two hours of screaming, flailing and crying were not normal. At the time, I thought it must be the prematurity or that her nervous system was underdeveloped. It would be years later before I understood.

I remember talking to the occupational therapist about Allie when she was about eight months old. Allie had stopped using her right arm and leg as much. She was relying on the left side more than normal. By the time the therapist came out again, it had resolved itself. Once, when the speech pathologist had come out, she began putting food to Allie's lip and Allie began turning toward the side stimulated by the spoon, making a sucking motion; Allie would have been more than a year old at this time. I said, "Hey wait a minute, is she rooting?" The pathologist agreed that Allie appeared to be rooting but couldn't confirm. I asked why she would be doing a newborn reflex now. The speech pathologist said she would investigate and get back to me on it. By the time the therapist came back to see us, the rooting had extinguished again and she had no answers for me.

Several more months of therapy for the twins passed with fewer answers for Allie's behavior patterns. I struggled to keep my attention on the twins and provide the same attention to my boys who were adjusting to sharing their mother. The boys were growing, becoming more adventurous and the efforts of managing four children were challenging my strength and faith daily.

There was one day when I reached a near breaking point. Adam and Brennan were in their room playing. I stopped to check on them in between feeding, holding and rocking the twins. I tried to open their bedroom door but could only open it slightly. Brennan had toppled over all of his bookshelves and they were blocking the door. He had also emptied every basket so that every toy, book, sheet, pillow was on the floor. Crying and screaming, Adam had climbed onto the only standing piece of furniture, a clothes dresser. He was again, in nothing but a diaper, but I couldn't get to him to help him. Through the crack, I noticed the bedroom window was open, so I left the house and went around to the outside of his room. I yelled at Brennan to get those things out from in front of the door so that I could get Adam down from the dresser. I was livid, my poor Adam needed me and I couldn't get to him. I called my mother and said, "If you want to see your grandchildren live to see another day, you'd better get over here." I tried to explain the nature of the room that looked like an Oklahoma tornado had hit it. But she didn't fully understand the depth of what they had done until she made it over and saw for herself. To my relief and surprise, she was angrier than I was at them. She was yelling much louder than I was to the point that I actually felt better. It wasn't my intent to feel better at her expense, but I think she honestly had never seen anything like it in her life. At long last,

Brennan cleared the doorway and I reached my crying, exhausted snotty-nosed child who had his pacifier hanging half way out of his mouth. He had been through quite an ordeal, and Brennan's ordeal had only just begun as my mother was barking orders at him left and right, determined to have him clean that room no matter how long it took. I was so grateful that she was there to help me handle that. When it's four against one, sometimes reinforcements have to be called in. Reinforcements were lifesavers for me as the four children aged. I was blessed to have an army of angels at my disposal when life became too much. Family and dear friends comprised a support group for me that would be relied on for babysitting, sanity checks and prayer time. God provides angels to those who love and honor Him. The "miracle twins", as they were commonly referred to throughout our small community, required constant attention. My patience, strength and faith were tested frequently. I prayed and prayed but there were many days when I, once again, just cried.

At three, Adam's speech therapy was taken over by the school system. He went 30 minutes twice a week to the school, while I waited in the car with the girls. I was prepared with enough bottles of breast milk, diapers and wipes to get us through the thirty minutes of speech that I had taken Adam to. In addition to speech therapy at the school, I had found the Tulsa Scottish Rite speech services and we went one time per week for an hour. Ms. Adrian, as we called her, was wonderful with Adam. Before they began play therapy each week, she would put Adam in a chair and help him to practice moving a fruit loop around his mouth, each time waiting longer and longer before he could bite down on the fruit loop. She also employed the use of spray candy and sponge-pops to help him gain awareness around his mouth and tongue and lips. At one point when Ms. Adrian asked Adam to put the 'sponge-pop' into his mouth, he took the 'sponge-pop' into his hand and tried to push it into his mouth through the skin above his upper lip and below his nose. I found this to be very odd and I asked Ms. Adrian if this was normal. She replied, "Yes, it is normal for children who are apraxic." Apraxic was a term I had become familiar with as a Soonerstart provider. I had actually seen a speech-delayed child who had been diagnosed with apraxia so I knew a little about it. Ms. Adrian began to explain that not only was Adam motor apraxic, but he was also oral-motor apraxic. He didn't know where his body was in space, any more than he knew where his tongue was in his mouth. Purposeful motor movements that were not already a part of his repertoire were excruciatingly difficult for him. This explained why he could not master new sounds on command. It was amazingly frustrating news. It wasn't as if Adam's therapeutic schedule would change, but more like a revelation that this wasn't something that would just go away. It meant that he might never learn to read, that he would continually have difficulty with writing, it meant that my second chance child would have a possible lifetime of academic difficulties at school. After all, reading and writing is the basis of learning at most institutions, at least I knew it was at the school he was going to be attending. We continued with Adam's therapies and even sought out occupational therapy for his motor apraxia and sensory integration difficulties. The girls were receiving their own therapy at home due to their extreme prematurity and now we were driving all over the place to get Adam the help that he also desperately needed. Brennan was in first grade at the time and he was having his own set of difficulties in school. I was completely overwhelmed. I often found myself in tears asking, "Why?"

So do not fear, for I am with you; do not be dismayed, for I am your God. I will strengthen you and help you; I will uphold you with my righteous right hand.—Isaiah 41:10

CHAPTER 7

—❧❀❧—

I had dreams and goals for myself as a professional. I had driven four hours a day, three days a week to Oklahoma State to finish my master's degree because I wanted to do things with my professional life. I knew I would likely never be able to work full-time as a Child Development Specialist with the responsibilities and the time demands of my children. One afternoon, the librarian at the elementary school where Brennan attended, approached me and said, "You know you could walk into any of the classrooms at this school and do as good or better a job being a teacher than what we have here all ready. Why don't you go get your teaching certificate?" It was the first time that I had seriously considered it. She told me that the state of Oklahoma had begun a program called the Alternative Placement Program. In short, it meant that if you had a degree in something, there was a process by which you applied, interviewed and passed the general education testing as well as your area of expertise and you would receive a teaching certificate. It was the best news I had heard in a while. I knew I could do it, I knew I had a love for children especially for those who had special needs or who were somehow seen as not as "lovable". I especially wanted to teach little boys who were active, busy and a little out-of-control—like mine. I knew we needed more teachers like that in the system, and I wanted to be one of those. My BA was in Psych and my MS in Family Relations and Child Development. The state considered my MS degree closely related to the Home Economics Teaching Certificate. I had to pass the Home Economics test before I could even take the Early Childhood test. Prayerfully, I commenced to studying for the test. The home economics test included sewing, interior design, cooking and child development. I knew a lot about child development, but little or nothing about the other sub-categories. I took the test and passed it and went on to pass both the General and the Early Childhood Tests. I received my teaching certificates in Home Economics sixth through twelfth grade and my Early Childhood Teaching Certificate. I was so excited. I immediately put my application in at my children's school. As God had done so many times in my life, He opened a window for me; there was a space available. I was thrilled to accept the position of kindergarten teacher and be at the school that my children attended, only five minutes from my house. It was an answer to prayer and I knew this is where God intended me to be. From day one, I began to notice children in my class who were exhibiting signs of being in need of special services. I was able to build rapport quickly with parents due to my extensive background in parent education. It was because parents knew that I loved their children, and only wanted the best for them, that I was able to make successful referrals for speech, OT and physical therapy for these children. In a short time, I decided to become certified in special education. I loved working with children and was especially drawn to children with special needs. I was amazed at how they could try so hard to be successful despite the challenges they had been born with. They were my heroes, just like my own children. My children struggled daily to keep up with their peers and to have school success. If they didn't have a teacher who loved them, they would begin to internalize their failures as a part of who they were. This was something I did not want any other child to experience. I was lucky enough to have children with special needs and to be a teacher of children with special needs and I know that this was exactly what God intended for me. I was happy, I was excited, and I loved my life.

There would be more struggles to come throughout my own children's education. I was a mother and a teacher at the school where my children attended. It was a delicate balancing act. I am certain that there were times that my co-workers thought I was a terribly mean person. It wasn't ever personal, it was my job. If I didn't advocate for my children, I was not sure anyone would. The fact that I lived in the district and was having to ask for services that would cut into an already stretched budget was never looked on favorably. Adam was my first mother-teacher conflict. It was not unusual for Adam to do things that would get him into trouble; he talked to himself sometimes in the cafeteria, he would say things that were not exactly table talk and would have stickers removed from his chart. Adam told the PE teacher one day when he was introduced to a jump rope that "PE sucks." This of course was true, being apraxic, he had no idea what to do with the jump rope. But Adam had to be taught specifically what he could and could not say at school. He was also an extremely picky eater and this often caused him grief in the cafeteria. He would go hungry if he wasn't allowed to get seconds on mashed potatoes, his favorite, until he tried everything on his plate. Adam's sensory integration problems precluded him from changing seasonal clothing in a timely manner. It was November and the Oklahoma weather had become predictably unpredictable and cold. Adam always preferred to wear slip-on shoes, clogs or flip-flops, even in cold weather. One cold day, the principal came to door of my room with Adam in tow. She said, "Mom, we are worried about Adam."

I asked "What happened?" The principal went on to say that Adam was still wearing flip-flops and that she and his teacher were worried that his feet would get cold on recess. At this point, I was almost relieved that we were only concerned about Adam's feet. I said, "Well to be honest with you, I don't worry about that. I refuse to dress my ten year old and if his feet get cold, he will change his shoes."

The principal at the time refused to let it go and went on to say, "If he doesn't begin wearing more appropriate shoes, he will not be allowed to go out to recess with his friends." Whether it was exhaustion or God giving me the sense to pick another battle, I restrained myself. I knew that in order to preserve my sanity there were some things about my children that I refused to fight with them about. Adam was an intelligent child that had the misfortune of living in Oklahoma where the seasons are dramatically different. Even in the extreme heat of summer, Adam would wear sweatpants and a long sleeve shirt. There are things that matter in life, and things that do not. At the time, Adam's shoes did not matter to me—or more importantly, they didn't matter to him. That evening, Adam and I had a talk. I told him that honestly I could care less what shoes he wore to school, but apparently his teacher and principal wanted him to wear tennis shoes and socks. I said, "You know that I love you no matter what, but I would really appreciate if you would wear socks and shoes to school so that I do not have to get another visit from my principal and so that you will be able to play on the playground at recess."

He looked at me with eyes that seemed very wise for a ten year old, he looked down and said, "Okay momma, I will wear socks and shoes to school."

Another incident was when Allie and Emma were in their second year of kindergarten. They had a different teacher from their first year and I was directly next door to their room. The girls were still speech-delayed and the speech pathologist at the school felt that it was best that they were not in speech together. It was not a problem for me either way, her seeing them with other children their age or together, really did not matter to me. What did concern me was that they were being pulled out of class during the thirty minutes of direct instruction time. The thirty minutes during the day that new concepts, letters, sounds and numbers were being introduced. I knew that this was their last chance to refine their reading skills, to be ready for first grade where there were desks and spelling tests. I was certain that they had no business being pulled out for speech therapy during direct instruction time. I made my concerns known to their teacher who I hoped would advocate for them without me having to be involved. She met with the speech pathologist and they both decided that it would be fine for the girls to be pulled during direct instruction time. The teacher assured the therapist that she would be re-teaching those concepts throughout the day. I was not convinced. I went to the therapist and told her my concerns. I suggested that, if she was just completely booked at all other times, perhaps we could do it before school. I had to be there at 8:00 a.m., she was there at 8:00 a.m. and possibly that could work for her. She said that would not be a problem. I went back to my room feeling confident that I was able to resolve that problem without anyone getting their feelings hurt. However, the therapist and my principal had a conversation about my girls and they had decided that 8:00 a.m. would not work. I received another visit from the principal in my classroom. She stated that we just needed to have an IEP (Individualized Education Program) meeting and get all concerns out into the open. She stated that 8:00 a.m. would not work for the therapist and that we needed to discuss the possibility of pulling them out during direct instruction. The mother bear in me took over, I said, "I do not want them pulled during direct instruction." We scheduled a meeting time and I told my husband he needed to be there. I was sure that being employed at the school was working against me and I thought if he voiced his views in an IEP meeting that maybe they would understand that we were not going to back down. The meeting was attended by the principal, speech therapist, the children's teacher, me and my husband. My husband finally spoke up and said that he did not want his girls pulled for speech services during direct instruction and the matter was settled. The speech pathologist found other times to pull them and we were good to go as far as that was concerned. It would however put a huge wedge between me, the speech pathologist and my principal that would not soon be healed. It was a difficult year, but I knew I had done the right thing. I needed to be sure that my children, all four of them, received the best chance they could in order to become successful in school. I let many things go that year in regards to therapy, because I knew we all needed to heal from the experience. I am grateful that God gave me the strength to stand up for my children when it was necessary, and that He helped me to allow some things to just fade away. Anyone going through these experiences might have a tendency to keep their fists raised and ready to fight at the least little things. I am one of those people, I have to admit it. However, it is through Christ alone that I am able to see through the clutter of crazy that surrounds this life. It is He who helps me continuously to let go of those things that don't really matter. Do I mess up? All the time, but I know that I am forgiven and that my intentions are pure. Are there times when I want to take the parents of the children in my class and help them become better educational advocates for their children? All the time. Do I get sick to my stomach, when I know that I have done everything I can do as a teacher of this child who has special needs knowing that this child has a right to certain things but going any further will be crossing the line? All the time. Have I had to sit and listen at staff meetings about how much money has been cut by the state for education and then go in to the Superintendent's office and tell him that my daughter needs more therapy on her hand? Yes. If God is on my side in this life and if He is for us can no man stand against us? Yes.

> *Be strong and courageous. Do not be afraid or terrified because of them, for the LORD your God goes with you; he will never leave you nor forsake you." 1 Corinthians 16:13*

CHAPTER 8

Life is full of mysteries, coincidences and curveballs. But I've always believed that God has a plan and it's not always my job to figure out the plan. This is a hard concept for someone who likes to be in-the-know about most aspects of life. In my first year of teaching, God brought an angel into my life named LeAnn. LeAnn and I had met on a vacation with mutual friends and bonded instantly. LeAnn and I shared a love of children, a love of laughter, a love of teaching and a love of God. We spoke often and as we learned more about each other, we found more areas where we were connected. LeAnn's daughter, Haven, was an in-utero stroke survivor. Haven was born with special challenges and frightening moments that I could relate to. LeAnn was strong and positive and someone that I could talk to about fears and hopes. God brought her into my life as an Angel and then took it one step further. LeAnn was interested in working part-time and I was interested in having a teaching assistant in my classroom. Once again, God provided a window and we both knew this was another gift of grace with perfect wrappings.

LeAnn and I worked together wonderfully. We loved the children and loved our jobs. I was amazed at her patience and sweet disposition. She was amazed at my positive attitude and the fact that I smiled a lot. She asked me once how I was able to be positive every day and greet each child with a smile and a hug, no matter what was going on in my life. I told her that I could be the only positive thing in a child's life. I could be the only hug or smile they received all day. I might not be but I wasn't willing to take that chance. God knew that

LeAnn would play a very important part in my life and in my future. He never fails to amaze me.

There was never a dull moment with the two of us combined and twenty kindergartners who often left us in tears of laughter. When my stepfather passed away, it was LeAnn who was there for me with the right words and the right understanding, because her father had passed away just a year before. God knew that I needed friends in my life that understood me and would be there for me in any circumstance. He knew this and He knew that these friends would be so important very soon.

It was a Friday afternoon at the school. We were picking up Allie and Emma at the office where they would wait after getting a ride from mother's day out. We took the girls back to the classroom and suddenly LeAnn asked, "What happened to Allie?" At first I assumed LeAnn was noticing her bruises from falling off the swing set at school so I explained what had happened. LeAnn said she had noticed a difference in the way Allie was walking and it didn't appear to be from a normal limp. LeAnn again asked about Allie and said that it did not appear to be a limp caused by a bruise or sore knee from a fall. LeAnn knew there was "a disconnect" when Allie was walking. I was skeptical at first, but I knew LeAnn loved my girls and I trusted her instincts. We made Allie walk across the classroom and it hit me; she was walking exactly like LeAnn's daughter, Haven. Her right foot was dragging with each step yet there appeared to be no pain. LeAnn had seen this many times with Haven and examined her leg more closely. LeAnn was concerned and so was I. There had been other signs as well that I began to discuss with LeAnn but I was certain that this was not the same as Haven. We agreed to watch her more closely as we packed up and left for home.

The next day I was painting Allie's fingernails and noticed that she could not raise her right arm. Her speech appeared to be more distorted and suddenly the panic that no parent should ever deal with hit me full force. I backed away from the table and asked Allie to raise both arms. Emma joined in and was able to raise both arms with ease. Allie could not raise her right arm off the table. I called my husband over to the table and showed him what I was seeing. I told him about what LeAnn saw and about the speech issues. "I think she's had a stroke," I told him. Donald began to cry. We hugged and I told him

I was taking her to the doctor. I was terrified but I knew I had to be strong.

It was Saturday so the doctors' offices were closed. I took the time to look up Pediatric Neurologists in Tulsa. A name I recognized popped up and I remembered his name from working with children who had special needs before I had children of my own. I took Allie to our local "Immediate Care" facility in Claremore, about ten miles away. "What's going on with Allie today?" they asked.

"I think she's had a stroke," I tearfully replied.

The receptionist left and returned to say, "If you think she's had a stroke, you need to take her to the emergency room in Tulsa." I hated emergency rooms, they were crowded with sick people and I only remember endless waiting—especially on the weekend. But, I gathered my baby girl and drove the 30 minutes to Saint Francis Children's Hospital in Tulsa. As we checked in, I noticed they prioritized her immediately and we got right in. She stood, a little wobbly, to be weighed and they inserted an IV to which Allie had no reaction. At four years old, she weighed in at only thirty pounds. They moved us to a room within the ER where we waited for a doctor to see us. We were watching a children's show on television in the room. I had called my mother and LeAnn on my way to Tulsa and they had rushed there as well. LeAnn's instincts were right. She knew that something didn't look right about the way Allie was walking. She was frantic about it, but at the time, I had dismissed it. Now here we were, waiting on the results of the CT scan. Something in me kept saying 'She is fine, they are going to let us go home after they do the CT because she is fine and there really isn't anything wrong with her that won't go away by tomorrow'. I looked over at the chart that had been placed to the side of the nurse asking questions—it read "Patient did not react to IV placement." I knew then that something was wrong.

The doctor came in and immediately said, "Well something is definitely going on with her. It looks like she has had a stroke. But there are older strokes that are present as well. We can see those on the CT scan. We will need to get an MRI to get more information. We are admitting her until we can figure out what is going on. The pediatric neurologist will need to see her." It was surreal, his words going over and over again in my mind. I began to cry and stroke Allie's arm. She was looking at me crying, not speaking, just looking at me, and watching me cry. I could tell it was starting to worry her, so I pulled it together and I started saying, "It will be fine baby. It's okay, you are fine."

My mom turned to me and said, "It will be okay, we will get through this."

I began to pray, "Dear Lord, give me the strength for what is to come. I cannot do this without you." I prayed knowing that I had asked Him just four years ago to let me have her and her twin sister for a while. I began to wonder if He was deciding that my time with her was up. I looked at LeAnn and said, "So, you think three or four days tops and we will be back home?"

LeAnn shook her head and spoke from experience. She said, "No. You are done with school. You will not be back this year." I was hearing it but not believing it. She said, "Your four year old daughter has had a stroke, and they don't know why. She has had many strokes from years past. You are done with school this year. I will finish the year out for you. Don't worry about anything. Trust me, hospitals are lonely, scary places and you are going to need each other to get through this. Focus on Allie, she needs you now. I will take care of everything at school."

Nineteen four-year old students were depending on me to finish the year for them, but I wasn't going to be able to do that. My daughter needed me right now, and here I would stay, by her side until she no longer needed me. God had placed this amazing friend and teaching assistant in my room from the beginning for a reason.

We made all the phone calls to friends and relatives and the school. They needed to know that I would not be returning that year. I had to make arrangements. My other three children had school tomorrow. I had to find someone who could take them to school and bring them home if possible. Donald was on night shifts at work at the time. I also had to find someone to watch them in the evenings until we got home. I was certain that would be soon, I was certain of it. I just kept saying, "She's four!!! Four year olds do not have strokes!! What is going on???"

We were admitted to the PICU at Saint Francis Children's Hospital. They told me that the pediatric neurologist had been notified, but he was out of town. The next day was Sunday and she appeared to be getting better. She was walking around the room, looking out the big window at the parking lot. Emma, her sister, came up and they played in the room and watched "SpongeBob" and "Dora". Nurses and doctors would come in to check her and seemingly looked surprised. This little girl who had had a stroke, numerous strokes, looked normal. They sent in an Occupational Therapist and a Physical Therapist to evaluate her. She looked so beautiful and so normal. The next morning was a different picture, a different Allie. We had been in the hospital for two days. Allie looked terrible. She wasn't talking anymore, wasn't walking around and couldn't even hold herself up. The anger inside me was building. I told the doctor that came in to check on her, "We are just sitting here watching her deteriorate! When are we going to do something about it?" He kept assuring me that the doctor had already reviewed her scans and was going to meet with me sometime that day. That brought me little consolation when I continued to watch my bright blue-eyed baby girl turn from active and playful into a complete zombie. I prayed constantly; not the make-an-appointment-get-on-your-knees with hands folded for a few seconds praying. It was the unceasing prayer of someone in complete and total crisis mode. I prayed constantly that day and for many to come. I prayed for strength, courage, and help. I prayed for healing of my baby girl, quick healing. But I also knew that if He had decided to take her, I needed to be thankful for the time He had given me with her. So I also prayed many prayers of thanks. I was extremely thankful to God that He had allowed me to get to know this amazing little girl for four years. It was more than I could have imagined. But of course, I wanted more.

And we know that all things work together for good to them that love God, to them who are the called according to His purpose.
Romans 8:28

That evening around 9:00 p.m., the doctor came into our room. He was a tall man, skinny with an amazingly caring and compassionate demeanor. He apologized profusely for the delay in meeting us. He said he was the only pediatric neurologist in the area, worked ridiculous hours, and just wanted to see his son graduate from college. I assured him that it was okay, no apology necessary. I really felt that he was going to do something to help her; that he knew what was going on and how to fix it and that was what he was here for. That was my prayer.

The doctor went over the results of the MRI. Allie had suffered a stroke which covered the left side of her brain. This accounted for the right-sided weakness and the lack of speech. He also discussed the possibility that she had been having strokes for years. There were "older lesions" he said, older areas of the brain that had been damaged from stroke activity. Dating back to when, he couldn't say, but years for sure. He then went on to say that she needed a test called an arteriogram. He only trusted a couple of people to do the procedure on a small child Allie's age. This test, the arteriogram, would run a catheter from her leg into her brain. A pediatric interventional radiologist would oversee the procedure and would fix, if possible, anything that he could see that was disrupting the flow of blood to her brain. Where this disruption was, he did not know, could not guess, but there was definitely a disruption somewhere. The pediatric interventional radiologist was in Fort Worth, Texas. We would be transported there in the morning as soon as possible. If insurance would cover it, we would be transported there by their emergency air-flight transport. Nothing by mouth in the morning, nothing until they had seen her; on top of everything else I had to explain to my four-year-old that I could not feed her when she was hungry.

As we sat in the hospital room in Tulsa, we made the phone calls to friends and relatives to let them know we were being sent to Cook Children's Hospital in Fort Worth, Texas. My principal brought up an envelope filled with VISA pre-paid cards and calling cards and about $400 in cash. They had sent an envelope around the school at Justus-Tiawah and they had collected all of these donations to help us with our expenses. It was the first of an amazing outpouring of God's love and blessings upon us. We waited for them to get the go-ahead from our insurance company, when a doctor came in and said, "Just get ready to go, they are on their way here to get you. They don't care if your insurance approves it, they will donate it if they have to. She is emergent, and they refuse to wait to hear if you have approval from your insurance company." God was indeed taking care of Allie. I closed my eyes and thanked my Lord Jesus for everything He had done for her. And as I was praying, I asked for one more bit of strength for me.

Flying or driving or any kind of motion when I wasn't behind the wheel was something that had been an issue with disgusting results for much of my life. I was not about to think only of myself in this case but the fact is to this day, I get car sick and air sick. Big commercial jets don't seem to bother me much but little planes, helicopters and car rides on long roads with lots of curves create a real problem with whatever my last meal was. Air sickness has hit me at some very inopportune times—on vacation in beautiful Napa Valley, on a helicopter ride above the Grand Canyon and on a romantic helicopter ride around the majestic falls of Maui. I knew the chances were good that a little afternoon turbulence on the way to Fort Worth, from Tulsa, would make me sick. I kept quiet about my condition because I knew that if they thought I got air sick, they wouldn't let me on the plane with my baby. I couldn't let that happen. She wasn't talking, couldn't walk or move her arms much. She could smile but only with the left side of her face and she couldn't even hold herself up. I had to be with her. The alternative was me driving there from Tulsa which would take no less than six hours. This would mean that she would arrive at the PICU in Fort Worth several hours before me and that was simply not acceptable.

I made my way to the gift shop on the first floor and bought two packages of Tums and a bottle of water. I was determined to make the 45 minute flight and not get sick. I wasn't able to bring any type of luggage on the plane. We boarded the plane; just me, my baby, my purse and my Tums. My husband had a friend from high school that offered to drive him to Fort Worth that day. This was another constant blessing from God; the blessing of good friends, friends that would drop everything to do something for us. I also had a friend from high school who offered to let me borrow her laptop computer. I hadn't talked to her in years and yet she was willing to let me fly to Texas with her laptop. I was stunned but so grateful. The laptop would help me to stay in touch with friends and family as no cell phones were allowed in the PICU. I couldn't believe how blessed I was.

I ate the entire roll of Tums before we finally landed. Everyone was very kind on the flight and they made sure that Allie could see me even though she was on the stretcher and I was sitting up, glued to the window of the plane. I knew that looking at the inside of the plane or at my daughter, who was looking at me, was certain to make me sick. It was incredibly windy at the landing sight. As they were taking Allie off the plane, her entire medical chart blew all over the airfield. EMT's in their blue flight suits went running everywhere trying to retrieve all that they could of her medical history. From the small airport, we loaded up into an ambulance and made our way to Cook Children's Hospital in Fort Worth, Texas.

At the time, my biological father, "Grandpa Chuck" was living in Austin, Texas. When he heard we were being flown to Fort Worth, he immediately loaded up his motor home and headed north towards Fort Worth. He sent me a text message at one point to let me know that he was there and they were all waiting for us. I was comforted by that. I really had not spent much time with him growing up and had only heard terrible things about him from my mother but there he was, he was there for me and for Allie, and I was comforted. My mother was not.

My mother and father divorced when I was eight years old. My mother remarried a man twelve years older than her named Ken, who was a very gentle soul. He was a Godly man, who left the raising of my sister and me to my mother. Rarely did he ever try to discipline us; he stayed back and let her handle us. I remember distinctly that after my parents' divorce I wore my hair in pony tails. I refused to wear it any other way for the next six years throughout all of elementary school through the beginning of junior high. I was known as the girl with the "pigtails". Sometimes, mother would make me wear my hair down for pictures, but you could still see the humps that were left in my hair from wearing it the same way for years. My biological father remarried a woman much younger than himself. My biological father, Chuck, and his wife, Kathy, were in the Army. They moved around a lot so my sister and I didn't visit much. My father got two weeks with us in the summer and every other Christmas. Mom would make it extremely difficult to visit him. She hated him in a way I've never really seen someone hate another person. She didn't hide it either. My sister and I were not allowed to like him, much less love him. She would have preferred if he had just dropped out of our lives completely and left us alone. This was something she told us many times. It was interesting growing up with two dads. I called them both 'Dad' but never when they were in the same room. At my graduation from high school they were both there and I yelled, "Dad!" and they both answered—just one of many awkward moments. I was careful never to make that mistake again. I didn't want to hurt anyone's feelings.

My step–dad, Ken, passed away from pancreatic cancer in January 2007. He hadn't been feeling well and was being treated for a herniated disc. In November, at Thanksgiving, he didn't look well. In fact, he had a little bit of a yellow tint to the skin on his face. On my birthday, December 10th, 2006, I drove to their house and said, "Dad for my birthday, I want you to go to the emergency room. Something is wrong with you and I love you too much to let you be sick another day." He agreed, so mom and I drove him to Tulsa to the emergency room. He was very yellow in the face by now and I knew that it had something to do with his liver. He got in right away and was diagnosed the next day with stage four pancreatic cancer. He was dying. They said he could do radiation therapy but there wasn't much chance at this point that it would do any good. The cancer had already spread to his liver and was knocking on the door of his kidneys. My dad did one radiation treatment and opted for hospice. I tried to be at the house as much as possible for my mother. He constantly read from his Bible, watched the Christian programming on cable and prayed. He was in constant prayer, asking for strength and healing. I think he was more worried about leaving my mother than he was about dying. He was a strong Christian man that had always been in the best of health. As we prayed and held hands with him on his death bed at home, he took his last breath and left this earth to join his Father in Heaven. I was afraid to leave mom by herself in that empty house and I wanted to spend the night with her in my childhood home. It was surreal, sitting at his funeral, thinking "I am not seriously at my father's funeral; this is not really happening, is it?" But through it all, there was a peace about it, and God was constantly giving us all strength to get through it.

As we approached the hospital in Fort Worth, messages and calls from my mom became more and more livid. She was going on and on about how he was "never" there for us growing up and how could he possibly have the gall to show up at the hospital even before we got there. I said some more prayers for my mother's aptitude for forgiveness to kick in and a prayer again for strength as we entered the unknown world of the healthcare system in Texas. My stepmother,

"Grandma Kathy", was actually very involved in making the Texas healthcare system the standard that it was at the time. She was the Assistant Commissioner of Health for the entire State of Texas which meant she licensed and inspected all the hospitals in the state of Texas that were trauma centers. I took this as another sign from God that Allie was in good hands.

An entire medical team was waiting there for us to arrive. There were three doctors and no less than five nurses to lift Allie off the gurney and start the painful process of starting IV's, taking blood pressures, temperature, weight, and height. She was screaming as they tried to get an IV in and I began to think that I had made a terrible mistake. My dad, who always carried a book and a very large refillable soda cup with him wherever he went, had been a nurse for over twenty years. He put his book down and joined in the army of professionals who were holding Allie down to start these IV's on her. I watched through tears as they tried to start an IV in her neck. She was screaming and crying and all I could think about was that I couldn't comfort her and had possibly made a huge mistake. At that time, all I wanted to do was grab her and run as fast as I could out of that hospital. Instead I turned away from the vision of my baby's torture and immediately began to pray and ask God for reassurance that we were where He wanted us to be. They hadn't done this in Tulsa because there wasn't anything they could do for her there. They needed an IV port to draw blood from, as well as a port to give the heparin and the saline. As long as she was on heparin, a blood thinner for people who have had strokes, she had to have her levels checked every day by drawing blood and testing it for clotting. Finally things calmed down and she settled in with her IV's and monitors that seemed to be everywhere. There was a TV where she could see her favorite shows. She kept asking for french fries. The medical professionals kept telling me that she couldn't eat until the Speech Pathologist took a look at her and noted that she was able to eat without choking. I kept telling them that she had been eating just fine for the last three days, but they had to know it for themselves. I snuck her some applesauce while they deliberated and finally around 4:30 p.m., a Speech Pathologist showed up with a plate of "soft" foods. It was gross; blended banana and everything was smashed so softly that it was like baby food. The Speech Pathologist decided it was safe to give her food and noted it in her chart. My dad immediately went downstairs to the cafeteria and brought her back a huge plate of french fries and a ton of ketchup. Allie felt so much better as she ate her fries and watched television and rested. It had been a long day for all of us.

There was a little space against the wall where one parent could sleep in the room with their child. I set up camp there and they brought me blankets and a pillow. One of the neurologists had been in the unit when Allie first arrived and had heard her screams and cries as they were starting the IV. She had been to the gift shop and brought her a pink stuffed poodle and a purple stuffed poodle. She had heard she was a twin, so one was for her and one was for her twin sister. I had not experienced such compassion and love. This doctor didn't even know us, but she was touched by this little girl who was stuck in the PICU following her massive stroke.

A social worker came by and introduced herself. She gave me all of the information regarding the hospital and the surrounding area, including restaurants, hotels, and the Ronald McDonald House. The Ronald McDonald house was currently full, and I would need to call every day to see if they had any openings. Late that evening, my husband arrived with his friend Dale. My dad left, after Donald had arrived, to set up for the night in his motor home. I knew my dad would be there for as long as I needed him to be. Dale had been to the gift shop and had already gotten Allie some things; a baby doll, which Allie loved, some things to do while she was laying in the hospital bed, crayons and a notebook. Allie immediately caught the attention of everyone. It was like looking into the face of an angel with her blonde hair and blue eyes. She smiled that crooked little smile at everyone; didn't speak, just smiled at them. They were amazed at this little four-year-old girl who had survived a series of strokes that had left 30% of the left hemisphere of her brain damaged. This little girl, who couldn't speak anything but single words, couldn't walk or move her right arm, left them all speechless.

The cerebral arteriogram was one of the first requirements to determine exactly what was going on in Allie's brain. A CAT scan from Oklahoma only revealed that Allie had been having strokes for some time. The actual procedure had to be done at the Harris Hospital medical facility across the street. I accompanied Allie while my dad spoke to the unit Chaplain. One of the nurses was a former nursing student of my dad's when he had taught at the University of Texas. She was very reassuring and comforting, as was most of the staff. They introduced me to the "Care Pages", a website that you could journal daily and share Allie's condition with friends and relatives all over the world. They in turn could post words of encouragement along the way. I immediately signed up for it and began to post:

May 23, 2008 at 5:27 p.m. CDT, Hey guys here is the most updated information we have, although it seems to change all the time. The angiogram showed no Moyamoya (check the internet). This is good news. No brain surgery—YEA! We understand that the right front carotid artery is completely blocked but has developed what they call collateral arteries. Also, the back right carotid has formed a bridge to shunt blood from the back of the head past the front carotid artery. The left front carotid artery currently is partially blocked by a clot. Part of this clot has broken off which has caused the stroke in the left side of her brain. The stroke currently is affecting 30% of the left side of her brain. This explains the right sided weakness and the speech impairment. At this point, they feel like she has a dissected (inside artery wall torn away from outside artery wall) aortic artery. When your body has a tear, scrape—it sends clots in order to keep from bleeding to death. Her aortic artery has increasingly been clotting for years, which explains the damage to her right hemisphere that shows as very old small strokes. There continues to be danger of the rest of the clot breaking up and going into her brain to cause more strokes. They currently have her on IV heparin to help dissolve the clot, however, the clot could be there 2-3 more months from now (or it could grow from more clotting). She will be on long term blood thinners and will require much follow up. Tomorrow, she is scheduled for an EKG and a CT angiogram to determine just where and how bad the dissection in the arteries is. She has some options, if it is indeed a dissected aortic artery. They can lace a stent in the artery, bypass the artery or allow it to heal on its own with continued heparin. They attempted a pic line several tries today with no success. Even sedated from the angiogram, she was hitting the nurses and kept waking up, requiring versed (verr-said). Thank you for your prayers. We believe in the power of prayer and appreciate you all. We are blessed to have such a support system! Love, Deb.

When the doctors had come back and said, "No moyamoya, no brain surgery," I cried in relief. It was an answer to many prayers. They were going to take a look at her heart to see if that was the problem. I thought "open heart surgery beats brain surgery any day". Although of course, I didn't want her to have to have either, but if given a choice, I was certain that they had been doing heart surgery for decades longer than they had been doing brain surgery; at least that seemed to make me feel a little better.

The PIC line was another agonizing endeavor. They had just brought her back from a procedure where she was sedated. They brought in PIC line nurses that had been doing lines for more than twenty-five years, and yet not one of them could get a PIC line started on Allie. She was sedated, but she would wake up kicking and swinging her arms around, hitting anyone within reach. They worked on her for at least thirty minutes and finally gave up. They gave her another medicine that would calm her down, Versed (verr-said). This was given to her anytime she was throwing a huge fit and her blood pressure would get up to 260 over 190. They didn't want her having another stroke from the extreme fits she would throw, so they kept Versed handy just for those occasions. I found a calming in prayer and the loving words of people who were following our drama. The Care Pages website allows friends and family to post entries of support and prayers to us while we are in the hospital. We had four entries on May 23rd:

We Love You—Allie, we are praying for you. We hope you come home soon! We love and miss you all. From Kaylee and the Clymas.

A Gift from Sally Walker—Allie, I hope you can come home soon to ride bikes. Feel better. I know God is watching over you. Love, Sally Walker.

Allie we love you—Allie we love you and miss you. We can't wait to see you. You are in our prayers. Love Uncle Tim, Aunt Kim, Keenin, Colton, Corbin, Brennan and Adam.

To Allison Paige—Allie, Granny and Papa love you. Get well soon!

I sat in the chair most of the night, and in fact, found myself halfway lying beside her in her hospital bed. She wanted me as close as possible and because the wires were not long enough for her to sit on my lap in the chair, I found myself inching closer and closer to her in the bed. The hospital policy dictated that parents were not to "co-sleep" with their child. They had all kinds of reasons, most of which had to do with safety. I had to sign all kinds of paperwork that released them from all liability if something were to happen to my baby while I was snuggling her to make her feel better. Allie watched television most of the day. Her favorite part of the hospital experience was getting to eat breakfast, lunch and dinner in bed. Allie was covered with so many IV lines, one in each arm and two in her neck at one point and she could only move her left leg. She would raise her foot up to my face to stroke it, as if to say, "I love you mom." I would reach up and pat her foot, as it stroked my face and she would smile at me, that half crooked smile that was left from the stroke. She couldn't feed herself, so I had to feed her. She couldn't use either of her arms for anything, least of all for eating or coloring. Even going to the bathroom was a chore. They brought a little bedside commode in and I would help her take steps to the potty while making sure that all of her wires didn't get tangled up or stuck in the toilet for any reason. Then, I would get her back into bed, fluff her pillow and re-arrange her wires and her covers.

They were running all kinds of tests to determine the cause of the arterial dissection. They began to look at her heart. They ran a Cardio CT scan with contrast dye. This of course meant nothing to eat that morning, because she had to be sedated for it. That test revealed no abnormalities, with the exception of a slight discrepancy in the size of the top of the aorta and the bottom. Official results revealed nothing abnormal except she has a "funny looking aortic arch". We were released from Cardiology as her heart appeared normal. They continued to have her on IV heparin, which requires blood tests to reveal the clotting factor, which in turn lets them know how much or how little heparin to give her. We were moved from general population to an isolation room which had glass doors that we could close. The PICU was very noisy. Aside from the constant beeps and codes, there is all of the talking. Doctors talking to nurses, nurses talking to other nurses or patients, visitors talking to each other, and sometimes there was the terrible moaning or screaming of a child who was in terrible pain. If that didn't keep you awake most nights, the bright lights of the PICU would definitely do the trick. Thankfully, another answer to prayer, we were moved to a private room which adjoined a suite. God provided as He had done so many times.

The Chaplain who my dad had visited with had made arrangements for us to stay in one of the hospital's most closely guarded secrets. The suite was for VIP's or for patients who were very far away from home and had no place to stay. The suite was awesome. It had a bedroom, living room, a kitchen and across the living room was another door that opened directly into a glass enclosed unit of the pediatric ICU. It was like having an apartment off to the side of your daughter's hospital room. I kept thinking that one night I was going to have to try the bed out; Allie had other ideas. At four years old when you feel really bad, you want your mother. Dad is cool and all, but really all you want is your mommy. And so, the bed became a dream that would not be fully realized until my mother made her way down to Texas.

My dear friends Marti and LeAnn drove my mom and the kids down to Fort Worth for a visit. It was an amazing feeling to see my other three babies again. My dad was still at the hospital and my mother and he were on their very best behavior. Marti, LeAnn and my dad watched Allie for us, while Donald, my mom and I took the other three to the Fort Worth Zoo. It was so awesome; like we were a normal family, just on vacation visiting the zoo. I was so excited that I was going to get to spend the night in the hotel with my children. I love Allie very much, but I also missed my other babies so much that it hurt. It is literally like having your heart cut into two pieces, knowing that all four of them need you and you cannot be with all of them. We spent an amazing day at the zoo and then back to the hotel where they swam and we just snuggled ourselves into oblivion on the giant king-size bed. It wasn't all complete bliss; they did fight over who was going to get to sleep next to me, which made me smile.

The next day, we were back at the hospital and I was saying goodbye to my kids. This was extremely painful. Words cannot express the amount of pain I was in, physical pain that I felt directly in my chest, as if my heart was about to break. I remember carrying Emma to the car and putting her in her car seat while she was crying and screaming "No momma, I want to stay, don't make me go, don't make me go!" I was physically ill. No mother should have to choose between her children. No mother should have to hear the screaming cries of her four year old child as they drive away. I cried as I walked back to the hospital room alone, where my critically ill child was waiting anxiously for my return. I looked to the heavens; this time with more questions than prayers. God knew my faith was strong but God also knew my heart was breaking and my strength was fading.

Praise be to the Lord, to God our Savior, who daily bears our burdens. Psalm 68:19

CHAPTER 9

-&❀❦-

Almost a week and a half went by when Donald decided he needed to go back to work. He had applied for Family Medical Leave, which is wonderful, but is also unpaid leave. We knew we would need money to pay all of the hospital bills, and so he left to go back home and go back to work. I was relieved, mostly because my other three children had been shifted from place to place during this time. I knew my friends and family were being very kind to them and helping them not to worry, but they needed their home. This had been difficult on them as well with mom and sister gone. They needed to be able to sleep in their own bed, pet their own dogs and cats and play with their own toys. As much as I would miss the support of my husband, I was happy for my other three children. It was also time, if Allie would allow, for someone else to stay in the room with her while I got some sleep; someone by the name of "Memaw."

My friend, Laurie, who had loaned me the laptop, asked her mom if she would drive my mother's car down to Fort Worth, with my mother in it, while she drove her car down so they would have a way to get back; a complete and total act of unselfish love. Laurie was my friend from high school, but it had been at least twenty years since we had really been close. And here she was, driving my mother down to see me and my daughter at a hospital in Fort Worth, Texas. Many examples like this reaffirmed that the love of God is alive and well in the people that surround you. Never underestimate the ability of someone and the depth of someone's compassion when you need it the very most. Mom, Laurie and her mother made it to the hospital. I was again comforted that I had someone there who would support me. Knowing how my mother felt about my father and how I didn't need any more stress on my plate, he went back to Austin. I hated to see him leave but it was a relief knowing that there would be no drama between them while I was focusing on Allie.

They began to run a series of genetic and DNA tests to explain why Allie had been having strokes and why her carotid arteries were dissected. She was assigned a metabolic geneticist to check for a connective tissue or collagen disorder. She was still on the IV heparin, but her levels were stabilizing. The hematologist wanted to transition her from the heparin to a Lovenox injection blood thinner as soon as possible. Once weaned from the heparin, she could be moved to the floor or a transitional care facility where she could get rehab. She was in desperate need of Occupational Therapy, Physical Therapy and Speech services. She was receiving all of them now, but not as often as she would if she was on the floor. She was very limited in the activities she could do while hooked up to all of the machines. They did let her ride in a wagon from time to time for trips around the outside of the hospital and to the gift shops. Allie loved taking trips in the wagon. She especially loved shopping at the gift shop. It was funny how she would pick something out for herself, and then would commence to shopping for her brothers and her sister. The rooms on the floor would offer Allie much more freedom to move around. She could go to the playroom and participate in all of the structured activities the volunteers had planned for the day. She could also go to the cafeteria with us and eat, which was awesome. Best of all, she could go outside and soak up the sun. Living on a ranch, she loved being outside and playing in the grass and running around. She missed being outside and feeling the warm sun on her face, and frankly, so did I.

That evening, she was listening to Emma talk to her on the phone. She was still unable to speak much so Emma did all of the talking. Suddenly, and very surprisingly, out of her mouth came "Love you," to Emma. It was music to my ears. Not only had she not been able to say those words, but that she was saying them to her sister, who she missed terribly. Allie's smile persisted and the love she shared for her family was always present in that smile, in her eyes and in those few spoken words.

Beloved, let us love one another, for love is from God, and whoever loves has been born of God and knows God. 1 John 4:7

Amidst all of the talk of transitioning Allie to the floor or to inpatient rehab, we began to look into a possible inpatient rehab facility in Oklahoma. This particular rehab facility was located in Bethany, just outside of Oklahoma City. We were sure that this would be better for all of us. This facility wasn't a six hour drive, only two hours from Claremore and much closer to our friends and family back home. But we would hold every day as a blessing regardless of where we were.

The first time Allie went for Occupational Therapy and Physical Therapy in the gym on the first floor was a major challenge for both of us. She had a terrible time walking around, holding herself up, and it took everything that she had just to do a puzzle. Not a difficult puzzle, just a puzzle with inset pieces that had knobs on the top of them. She was learning how to use her left hand. She had always been right handed, extremely right handed and now she had to learn to use her left hand to do everything. I watched her struggle to pick up the pieces of the puzzle and hold herself in position; I started to cry. It was a helpless feeling watching my baby struggle to do things she had done all of her life. She loved the swing where she could lay on her stomach and hold on with her left hand for dear life. They kept trying to get her to use her right hand, but of course, that was where there was still an IV intact and she refused to use the hand where the IV was placed. She despised the ball pit. At one point she had a look of panic on her as she could not get upright in the pit, it was if she was drowning, not in water, but sinking into the unending pit of plastic colored balls. She was scared; she could not even lift herself out of a ball pit. I was sad for her, I felt bad that she had to work so hard. I couldn't let her know it though. It was my duty to stay strong for her, because no matter how sad I was feeling, she had to be feeling worse.

Allie's Genetic Metabolic Specialist sent blood samples to Washington D.C. to check for the collagen deficiency disorder and

Marfan's Syndrome. They continued to be baffled by her condition; it is extremely rare to have both of the carotid arteries dissect. Allie was continuing to do better each day she was there. She was beginning to be able to walk without any help, and she started using two word sentences to communicate. She would say things like "more bacon" and "I'm ready". She continued to struggle with direct questions that required more than a yes or no answer. If someone asked too many questions of her at once, she would just smile at them, her crooked little smile. Even her smile was getting better. Unless she was tired, she almost had a full smile. She smiled at everyone. Even the doctors who weren't on her case came in to talk to her and play with her. Everyone was so taken by her. They were all in awe of this little girl who was doing so well despite her obvious brain damage from the strokes.

Apparently the awe that was shared for Allie wasn't confined by the walls of the hospital. We had numerous friends and acquaintances, even people we didn't know, who were sending Allie care packages. She would receive an entire box full of snacks, a new dress, a toy or a new doll from people all over the country. Sometimes, they would just send cash or gift cards to the Starbucks in the hospital. She loved getting mail. Her face completely lit up every time she got a piece of mail with her name on it. We got an amazing amount of cards offering words of encouragement and support. Many of the cards had Bible Verses. All the individuals who wrote on the "Carepages", sent cards, or care packages, all of them were praying for us. They would tell us about how not only were we on their church's prayer list, but on several of their friends' prayer lists. We were on prayer lists in almost every state in the country. My father-in-law, who is catholic, went to the monastery near where we live and asked the monks to pray for us. We were being protected, cradled, loved, and supported by hundreds of people. They were going to God on our behalf. God was answering their prayers, every day that Allie was still with us. Every day that my little girl was able to walk, talk, hold my hand, eat bacon, and smile at everyone; every day was an answer to our prayer, and the prayers of others. Every time we got a card, a care package or just a note of support, I wanted to make sure they understood how much we appreciated it. I would write thank-you cards by the hundreds, made calls, wrote things like: "We LOVE, LOVE, LOVE you all" and

"Thank you so much for your support, you all are taking such good care of us. We love and miss you all." I would write things like "We appreciate all of your prayers" and "We are so blessed to know each and every one of you." It was an outpouring of love and support for Allie so strong that I had honestly never seen anything like it. In fact, I was certain I didn't deserve any of it. I couldn't deny my daughter the prayers and support she desperately needed, so I accepted each and every gift, card and caring words. I never fully felt comfortable with it. I wanted so much to know each of them by name, to be able to thank them by name. In fact, while we were in Texas, the maintenance base at American Airlines had a benefit hot dog dinner for Allie. The Crew Chief from Donald's seat shop brought us the check. They had made more than $2,000 for us. It was amazing. I couldn't believe it. There were so many names on that card that I couldn't begin to thank them all.

Another blessing from God came soon after that. Allie was off the Heparin and on the Lovenox injections. She was moved to the floor where we were all so much happier. Grandpa Chuck had bought Allie a brand new bathing suit so she could play in the "splash pad" in the grass beside the hospital. Cook Children's Hospital was amazing. They had a beautiful playground that was just outside the hospital front door. Within the playground was a splash pad, which Allie absolutely loved. She had been down there once before, but only for a short time. Knowing we might be discharged to inpatient rehab on Monday, Donald had brought the children down again for a weekend visit. Both Allie and Emma put on their bathing suits and headed out to the splash pad. They had the best time. They were inseparable, they hadn't seen each other in more than a week and it was obvious that each one was desperately missing the other. This experience was the first time they had ever been separated, the first time that Emma had ever been without her mother. It was something that none of us could have possibly planned for and certainly not anything we expected. Allie would get her lunch tray and both the girls would sit on the bed and eat. While eating in bed, they would watch the movie "Enchanted". This movie was one of those that was shown four times a day and throughout the night on the hospital movie channel. Allie knew all the songs in the movie and would often sing them at the top of her lungs, both in the PICU and on the floor. Allie and Emma were also able to play in the playroom, where there were tons of toys, puzzles, books and video games to play. On that particular day they had music therapy. Both girls were given an egg shaker to shake along to the live music that two men played and sang to. Allie loved music therapy. She shook her shaker egg like a mad woman with her left hand. Allie and Emma loved pulling her wagon around the floor and running. We were always terrified Allie would fall, because on the Lovenox, her blood wouldn't clot if she got hurt. But we didn't deny her the pleasure of playing with her sister who she loved and missed so much.

The doctors and nurses at Cook Children's Hospital were so caring and friendly. As a parent, I was always included in the care of my child. I was included when the nurses gave "report" at shift change, I was allowed to ask questions or give input at any time during her care. Once moved to the floor, the care was no different. They were amazingly kind and began instructing us on how to give Allie shots in her tummy; Lovenox is given in an injection into the stomach. The needle is not small, about an inch and a half in length and she was not happy at all about the new way to get her blood thinner in her body. Lovenox is a very expensive drug as well and we had already been in touch with our pharmacy at home on how much we would be out of pocket for the month. On Lovenox, like Heparin, Allie's blood levels had to be monitored daily. Allie was given a Lovenox shot in the morning and her blood clotting levels were measured four hours from the time the shot was given. This time frame gave the most accurate reading of her particular levels. The Hematologist wanted her levels to be between .5 and .6. The Saturday before we were supposed to be discharged, her blood clotting levels shot up to .9. This was dangerous, because it was possible with levels that high, to have a brain bleed. They skipped her shot the next morning and checked her levels again. They also wanted one last CT scan before they released us to drive to Bethany, Oklahoma for inpatient rehab. As always, Allie wanted me to stay right beside her at all times. She didn't even want me to update the "Carepages"; she would whine and cry for me to be right beside her. In her bed, in fact, was exactly where she wanted me to be at all times. Thankfully, my mom was still there with me. She was sleeping on the reclining chair and I was in Allie's bed most of the time. Even when I tried to get out of the bed in the middle of the night, she would wake up. If she couldn't find me or see me right away, she would start to throw one of her famous fits that would require a sedative, so I tried to stay as close as possible. I was exhausted. I had not slept in a bed in more than thirteen days. I hadn't slept an entire night for more than seventeen days. I was on autopilot. Every time she did a little better, I would pray and say, "Thank you, Lord Jesus, for giving me one more day with my little girl. I know I don't deserve it, but I am so grateful that you have let her be here with us this day." When Allie would take a turn and not be smiling, or walking as well, I would pray, "Dear Lord, Heavenly Father, please bless sweet little Allie Paige and give me the strength to be strong for her. Help me to be a good strong mother to her, help me to be here for her whatever she needs me to be." I really looked at each day I had with her as a gift; a gift of grace. I had learned by now to not question the wrappings but to appreciate the gift.

Allie had her CT scan, Lovenox injection and blood drawn the morning of June 2, 2008. We were finally being released from Cook Children's Hospital in Texas, to drive ourselves to The Children's Center in Bethany, Oklahoma. The Children's Center was the only place in Oklahoma where they were equipped to handle children with medical and therapeutic needs. The Center was staffed with nurses, doctors, music therapists, speech/language pathologists, physical therapists, occupational therapists and a couple of doctors who were available and on-call 24/7. We were lucky to find one closer to home than Fort Worth, Texas. The Children's Center allowed for one parent to spend the night in the child's room, and provided one meal a day to the parent. There was an onsite playroom equipped with puzzles, books and toys whenever Allie wanted to play there. There was coffee and tea available all hours of the day and night. There was also a place in the center of the building that was outdoors and contained a rabbit and a turtle as pets. The children were allowed to feed the bunny and the turtle at certain times of the day. They also had available a playground equipped to safely accommodate children with special needs. They even had swings that would hold a wheelchair. It was an amazing place. A definite blessing, an oasis in a desert in which we felt great relief to be back in our home state.

Mom drove us most of the way from Fort Worth to Bethany. We stopped many times along the way because Allie had to "go to the bathroom". We had her favorite CD on in the car and she was trying very hard to sing along with it. If it was a slower paced song she could do it, but anything that had a beat or quick tempo, she would get lost in all the lyrics and the tune. It was extremely difficult to hear her sing. My little girl, who had the voice of an angel, always on tune and always on beat, could not keep up with her favorite songs. I wanted to cry, but I just kept telling myself, she is young, she can get it back. The brain is like plastic when you are under the age of seven. What the stroke had damaged was dead and would not come back. The brain in a child has the ability to re-route nerve cells and make new connections, hopefully to allow Allie to regain the use of her hand. I prayed she would eventually use other parts of her brain and get all of her skills back.

We switched drivers half way through and I drove us in to the Children's Center at Bethany, Oklahoma. As we entered, they came to greet us; they had been expecting us. Donald met us there at the center and helped us get settled in. As we were getting acclimated to the new place, Allie fell while running around the room and hit her head. Immediately, everyone went into panic mode. The Doctor in charge came in and very nicely told us that she would have to stay in bed the rest of the day to ensure that she hadn't damaged anything on or in her head. Needless to say, she was not happy. Also adding to her despair was the fact that no matter how much progress we had made since the stroke, each hospital or care center had to do its own evaluations of her. So again, she was presented with a tray of pureed foods. The speech/pathologist had to evaluate her ability to chew and swallow without difficulty before releasing her to eat solid foods. I explained to them that we had already been cleared for solid foods in Texas and on the way had stopped at a local restaurant where she had eaten a burger and fries; that didn't matter. What mattered is that they had cleared her personally and were not liable if she choked. We stayed in bed that day. She was asking for "SpongeBob". We looked up at the television which carried only local channels, no cable, and there was no VCR or DVD player. Of course, Allie's daddy ran right out and found a local store and purchased the cheapest DVD player he could find, along with a "SpongeBob" DVD. She was a happy girl.

The next day, June 3, 2008, the nurse came in and gave Allie her Lovenox shot and drew her blood to check her levels. She had been cleared to eat a regular diet, and the Occupational Therapist, Speech/ Language Pathologist and Physical Therapists would be coming in today to do their evaluations of her. They had a gym with all kinds of equipment for children with special needs to utilize in order to strengthen their muscles and their balance. Allie's personal favorite was the platform swing. She loved lying on her tummy and holding on with all of her might, while the therapist pushed her back and forth. Because of the fall she had taken the night before, they decided that if she was up and moving, she needed to have on a waistbelt. A waistbelt is a belt about six-eight inches wide and goes completely around her waist. It gives a person something to grab onto in case she begins to fall. Allie hated her waistbelt. It is actually called a "gait belt". She hated it. The therapists were immediately in love with Allie. Allie just had a way about her, she smiled all the time and if she didn't want to do something for you, she would smile almost to say, "Can I get out of it?" She disliked the foam pit almost as much as the "gait" belt. It was difficult for her to climb out of the foam pit. Being initially strongly right handed, the muscles in her left hand were not very strong and now, she only had those to rely on. Not to mention that her legs were also weak and she had to work with all her might to get out of that pit. Of course, the therapy was good for her, but it was difficult too. It was very hard for me to watch. I prayed for her pleasant temperament and strength to continue, mine as well. I prayed that she would continue to capture hearts with her smile and that she would continue to hold a positive outlook on everything she had to go through.

For God gave us a spirit not of fear but of power and love and self control. 2 Timothy 1:7

CHAPTER 10

The night of June 3rd would see an event that would change us forever. An event that God knew was necessary but, like so many other things, was a complete shock and total setback. Donald had been giving Allie Lovenox shots at the hospital and there had been no issues. I went to the library so I could update the care pages website and tell everyone about our day. When I returned, I could sense the tension immediately. Donald had started to inject Allie with the Lovenox but instead pulled the needle back out and said to the nurse, "I think this is too much."

"No," the nurse said, "we measured it and we always double check it. It is fine." Donald re-injected the needle into her stomach and gave her the rest of the Lovenox. The nurse departed with the needle and came back moments later with a panicked look on her face. "Oh, my gosh! You were right, it was too much." Now, I understand that doctors and nurses are people and people make mistakes; I get that. I cannot tell you what a blessing it was to us to have doctors and nurses involved in Allie's care who were brave enough to say, "I don't know" and "I made a mistake". Anything other than that would have only added to a nightmare that we could not wake from. Anything other than that would have been completely unacceptable and would have made for the possibility of anger which I had absolutely no time for. Panicked, the nurse again said, "You were right, it was too much." I immediately felt faint.

"I thought it was," Donald said. "How much too much?" he asked.

69

"Ten times her dose," the nurse said. They had misplaced the decimal point. The nurse was in tears now, I was in tears now and Donald was sick to his stomach. He had injected her with an enormous amount of blood thinner that could easily kill her. He had questioned it, but trusted that the nurse had measured it. He felt totally to blame. The nurse was in tears thinking she just allowed this little girl, the sunshine of the entire Children's Center, to overdose on her blood thinners, something that could kill her or cause her to have an enormous brain bleed which could lead to further stroke and debilitation. I was thinking, "Why did I leave them alone? I should have stayed and checked everything. I can't believe this is happening." While all of the bustling of professionals calling other professionals to find out what to do next, I dropped to my knees and prayed. I prayed that God would show us what to do from here, that somehow this would work to the benefit of Allie if at all possible, that He would give us all the strength and the humility to work together to find a solution to this problem without any defensiveness or blame, neither of which would have been productive at all. Because we live in a society where mistakes mean money, everyone at the Center was in a panic. I overheard another nurse trying to make this nurse feel better by saying, "Oh this is your first overdose in two years, wow that is pretty good." That irritated me. I went to the desk and asked to speak to the Doctor in charge. The nurse would not allow me to speak to him. I called the doctors that I knew at Cook Children's Hospital in Fort Worth and told them what had happened.

The Neurologist on-call was livid, "They did what?" he said. I told him that they were not allowing me to talk to the doctor in charge and I just wanted to know what they thought we should do now. He immediately called the number I had given him from the card the doctor had given me the day before. Immediately, I was involved again in Allie's care. The Neurologist from Cook called me back and let me in on what the plan was from their perspective. They believed that they needed to give her an anti-blood thinner to counteract the effects of the overdose. Driving her to the hospital by ambulance or otherwise was completely out of the question. Moving her even a little could result in death as she had no ability to clot her blood and the likelihood of her bleeding to death became all too real. Immediately, I was instructed to take a call from the desk.

The doctor in charge was aware that I had tried to talk to him and wanted to make sure that I understood the plan they were going to put into place to counteract the effects of the extreme overdose. They brought in their most experienced nurse to give the injection of the coagulant. Donald and I kept telling the responsible nurse who was still in tears that it was okay, that Allie was going to be alright. We tried to make her feel better but inside we weren't completely sure how all of this fell into God's plan for us and for her. We knew that making that this nurse feel badly was not in God's plan. It took them two and a half hours to locate a coagulant from a pharmacy that late at night. Unfortunately, the coagulant had to be given within a thirty minute time period and so with no IV in place, Allie endured thirty minutes of a needle in her arm and coagulant being injected for a ridiculously long thirty minute time-span, any faster and the blood at the injection site would clot and they would have to start all over. She did amazingly well although I had to help comfort her while she was crying. I was sick to my stomach. I couldn't believe that not only had she been through so much, but now, she was going through even more. I prayed for strength the entire thirty minutes I was beside her. I stroked her hair and head; I kissed her cheek and tried as best as I could to try to comfort her. It was nearing midnight and we were all exhausted. They took her blood to check her levels that evening after the overdose and while normal are between .5 and .6, Allie's blood clotting level was 3.6. By morning, it was down to 1.6 and we were on the downhill slide of one of the most scary and stressful evenings of our lives. She was on strict bed rest due to the risk of bleeding and was not able to do any therapy in the gym for the remainder of the day; an entire day, seemingly wasted because someone had missed a decimal point. But another day when God sent His heavenly angels to take care of Allie and keep her with us for one more day.

For he will command his angels concerning you to guard you in all your ways. Psalms 91:11

We had made several phone calls to close friends and family and asked them to pray for Allie that day. By June 5th, she was back up walking around and going to therapy. The social worker came in that morning to ask how we were doing. I started to cry and said, "We are fine, we are going to be fine." At the time, she had no idea why I would have said that and she went out to the desk to find out the story of what had transpired the night before. She was mortified. She felt so badly for us that she worked something out for us that would be another answer to prayer. She and the staff made arrangements for us to stay at the makeshift apartment inside the center. The apartment was there to help parents of children who were being discharged learn to care for them in a more realistic setting before being allowed to go home. It wasn't being used at the time and they offered it to us. It had a bed for a parent to sleep in, a living room and kitchen. Of course, we jumped at the opportunity that would allow Donald to stay there with us rather than having to find a hotel.

The Doctor in charge of the facility came by to check on us that morning as well. He knew what had happened the night before and was unhappy that they nursing staff did not let me talk to him. He apparently had a talk with them as he handed me his personal cell phone number and said, "That will not happen again, if you ever have any questions about Allie's care, you call me, no matter the hour." I couldn't believe it. I had never had any doctors hand me their cell phone number and seem to really want me to call him if I had any questions. Again, what had happened was out of our control and we were making the best of it. It was in Allie's best interest for us to all stay positive and keep a kind attitude, and so we did.

That day, Allie met with the Occupational Therapist who introduced me to what she called "limb restriction" therapy. Limb restriction therapy is where you restrict the good arm to increase the use of the "bad" arm. I trusted the therapist and knew that this would have been really good for her, but at the time I was thinking, "Are you kidding me? Do you have any idea what she has been through over the last three weeks? Do you know how much pain has been inflicted on her, how miserable she has been or how far away we are from our friends and family? How far away and alone we feel?" Of course, she didn't. She was young, fresh out of school, unmarried and without children. She was being reasonable and efficient. I wasn't able to see it from her point of view and she was unable to see mine. We took our quandary to the Doctor in charge. He agreed with me that frustrating a four year old while doing therapy with her was not going to work. We decided to primarily rely on games or play-based therapy to try to coax her into using her right hand and arm. She really had no use for it. The right arm and hand was in the way, it was a nuisance. She had little, if any, sensation in it and she certainly wasn't able to get it to do something for her. For the most part, she ignored that limb and started using her left arm and hand or her mouth or feet. Allie's speech was getting better but she still had a very difficult time answering questions. She would point and whine to get what she wanted because it was, after all, the fastest way to her goal. Some of the games and therapies were fun and some seemed more like work. Allie loved Music Therapy. She sang "The Wheels on the Bus" and the "ABC" Song and even got to play some instruments. After therapy, I was able to attend a staff meeting in which all of the therapists who were working with Allie discussed treatment strategies and decided when she would be able to go home. Their goal was to discharge her in two to three weeks.

Her schedule during the week was quite busy. She was in therapy of some sort for most of the day, Monday through Friday. On the weekend, things slowed down dramatically. June 6, 2008, Granny and Pawpaw brought Emma down for a visit. Allie completely perked up. She was elated that Emma was there with her. In fact, Allie tried to give Emma a kiss, but Emma wanted no part of it. They played for most of the day and I had to follow her around the entire time. I had to be holding on to her gait belt to ensure that she didn't fall and hurt herself while they played 'keep away' with a beach ball. The time I spent, watching them playing and laughing were some of the best times. They really helped me feel better. I began to envision an end where we just go on from here and put this experience behind us. I promised God that I would learn the lesson he was trying to teach me, but I was sure that I couldn't take too much more of this. But it was in times like those, I realized I was only human and had to completely rely upon Him for strength.

I can do all things through Him who strengthens me. Philippians 4:13

It was an amazing day with the girls getting to play together. Unfortunately, the time always came when they had to say goodbye and that time came very quickly. Granny and Pawpaw were ready to go home and Emma was not quite finished spending time with me and her sister. Donald decided that we would let her stay a little longer and that he would take her home with him when he left later that evening. Delaying the inevitable was difficult. On one hand, I was delighted to have Emma get to stay. I missed her dearly and desperately wanted us all to be together. On the other hand, she would have to go home some time and it was not going to go smoothly. That evening Donald and Emma left and, once again, Allie and I were alone. LeAnn had warned me that hospitals can be very lonely and scary—she was right. Allie and I snuggled up together on her bed and watched a couple of movies that had been brought to us from home. She fell asleep early and slept until well after noon the next day.

June 7th came and she was sleeping very late. I knew that she needed her sleep to heal, but I also knew that one of the signs of a stroke was sleeping afterwards. I dismissed it. Around 1:00, I took her with me to get a cup of tea. She had missed breakfast and she was eager for lunch. I walked with her out towards the counter where the tea was and I could tell she was weak. Her legs seemed to buckle under her and she was wobbly. We went by the cafeteria to gather carrots and celery to feed the bunny and the turtle. She kept saying, "I want to see the bunny." We found him and she was so happy. It wasn't long before she had that bunny on her lap and was petting it and feeding it carrots. When it hopped away to rest, her mind was on finding the turtle. After about ten minutes, we found the turtle, and fed him what we had left of our vegetables. Quickly, her attention and focus turned to finding the playground. She wanted to swing but she seemed unable to hold herself up on the swing so we just walked around the playground and looked outside the bars that were keeping us in the facility. It was then that I started to compare the center to a prison of sorts. She wasn't allowed to leave without being discharged and there was no way she would let me leave without her. I had to keep an eye on everything, watch everyone and measure all of her doses. I became the mother bear you hear about who comes out when their cub is in danger. That was me. I was determined to be her advocate, her protector, her security, and her support.

I decided that she was still acting weird. I just had a sense that something wasn't right. Back at the room, I let the nurse know my feelings, my fear that something was wrong. I was hoping that I was just being overly dramatic and protective. Unfortunately, every time they took her blood pressure, it was up, even though she was lying in bed. They decided that to be on the safe side, they should call the ambulance to take her to the nearest hospital. I suggested that I could drive her myself but they wouldn't let me do that; policy was that she was to be transported by ambulance. The ambulance was called and we began another stressful journey to the closest hospital. As I sat there with her in the ambulance, I just kept thinking that she would be fine. I wasn't ready to believe that it was possible she was having another stroke. I was also worried, that they wouldn't know what to do with her. I was hoping that surely in this big hospital in Oklahoma City they had a pediatric neurologist on-call that could consult with our pediatric neurologist in Tulsa about her case. I was also thinking about the possibility that nothing was wrong with her and I was putting her through this process again. What if I was wrong and she had to endure IV's, blood draws, CT scans and other painful and scary tortures? But even a worse thought—what if I was right?

We entered the emergency room and they immediately had me recite her medical history. I relayed the story about the overdose at rehab. They ran a CT scan and we waited. I called Donald and told him the situation. Donald said he would meet us at the hospital as soon as they knew she would be staying. We waited for what seemed tens of hours. I knew she was due a Lovenox shot that evening at 8:00. I watched the clock; 8:00 p.m. passed then 9:00 and then 10:00. Finally, we saw the emergency room doctor in charge and he was not happy. He came in where Allie and I were waiting and said, "Well, she has obviously had a stroke, but I can't tell if it is new. I don't have anything to compare it to." He was pacing a little bit and he appeared to be getting frustrated.

I said, "Her records are in Texas, do you want me to drive down and get them?"

He answered very short with me and said, "You may just have to do that." Now I was annoyed. I kept telling the nurses that she was past due for her Lovenox, and no one seemed interested.

I finally asked to speak to the Doctor and I told him, "Just discharge us and we will drive straight to Saint Francis Hospital in

Tulsa. They have records that they can compare a CT scan to and our doctor is aware of her case. We would feel better being in Tulsa." I was sure he would agree with my idea since they obviously didn't know her history and weren't doing anything for her at all. So again, I started to pray. I prayed that God's will be done for Allie; that He would give these doctors the wisdom to know their limitations and to release us to drive ourselves to Tulsa. At midnight, a full hour after I made my plea to the doctor, a nurse came in and said, "You are being discharged, we have called Saint Francis Hospital in Tulsa and they will be expecting you to arrive there two and a half hours after you leave here. However, we are going to put you in a room for right now and get you out of the emergency room until we can get you discharged." We were moved to a room shortly after midnight. As I watched the clock creep past 1:00 in the morning, I asked them to please give her a Lovenox shot. At almost 1:30 in the morning, the nurse brought the needle in to give Allie a shot. It was a different syringe; the measurements were different than the syringes they had been using at rehab. Still being in "momma bear" mode, I asked them to double check the dose. I called Grandpa Chuck for verification of the dosage; I wanted to make sure we didn't make another mistake. He said the dose was correct and so she got her dose of Lovenox. By this time, Allie was starving. They brought her a dinner tray and she proceeded to eat dinner at almost 2:00 in the morning. While waiting to be discharged, we both fell sound asleep. Honestly, we couldn't have left until Donald got there with the car, but I still couldn't wait to get out of there and back to Tulsa. Donald and my father-in-law arrived the next morning around 8:00. Allie was brought her breakfast and she was quietly watching television. We waited as doctors would stop in the doorway, look at her, point and talk and then walk away. Now we knew what it felt like to be the monkeys at the zoo. They'd never seen anything like her before and they all wanted to get a look at her. Her dinner tray from the night before was still sitting by the door, and before any semblance of a discharge began, we were able to add her lunch tray to the stack. I kept asking, "When are we going to be released?" They always answered, "We are working on that." I am a woman who rarely prays for patience. I knew that if I was to pray for patience, God would only present me with opportunities to practice patience. It was challenging to be patient knowing my little girl could be having another stroke. I immediately got on the Care Pages and told everyone that whoever was praying for me to have patience should stop immediately, instead, I would like to have prayers for strength, wisdom, knowledgeable doctors who are willing to admit when they do not know the answers, and a peace that passes understanding among all of us who are in charge of this precious baby girl. It was 4:30 in the afternoon and I was nearing the verge of a nervous breakdown, because I did not want to spend another night in this hospital. They brought her dinner and she finished it; another tray was stacked on the two previous trays when a nurse finally came in with our discharge instructions. I immediately began thanking God for the end to what I considered to be a very stressful two days. Not knowing is one thing that really drives me crazy and it is then that I have to rely on the strength of Jesus to help me get through those times. It is never easy and it is never fun, but He gets me through it and I look back at the experience and just say, "I sure wouldn't ever want to do that again."

After an eight hour delay, Donald, Allie and I finally began our trip to Tulsa. I had such immense relief go all over me. We were heading home. Perhaps this was all over, perhaps she hadn't had a stroke and this was our ticket out. We were not going back to Rehab in Bethany, it didn't matter what the verdict was where Allie was concerned. There had to be another way, some place, somewhere that she could get the same amount of therapy or close enough to it that we could go home; go home and be a family again.

There were several times throughout the experience that I thought if I could just wake up I would realize this was all just a bad dream. I kept thinking back to when it all started and I thought it would be great if this was all just one horrible nightmare. But it wasn't a dream, it was a nightmare and we were very much alive and living it. It was really happening to my baby girl. She was having strokes; she couldn't talk, walk or use her right arm. She had to relearn how to eat, draw, color, zip, pull, push, hop, jump, talk, and answer questions that didn't require a "yes" or a "no". This was really putting a strain on everyone I held dear. Friends and family were all stretched to the limit watching my children, bringing us meals, donating money and time to make sure we had everything we needed. This was really happening to Emma, unable to see her mom and her sister for weeks at a time. This was really happening to Brennan and Adam, worried about their sister, separated from their mother. My other three children had to spend the night with different people, different nights of the week, without being able to really enjoy their summer. It had to be a nightmare, but it wasn't. It was all really happening.

CHAPTER 11

$\rightarrow$ ✿ $\leftarrow$

After almost a three hour drive, we arrived at Saint Francis Hospital and went straight to PICU where they were waiting for us. Allie was scheduled for an MRI the next morning and so she could have nothing to eat or drink after midnight. They had an MRI machine that had a video headset so the child could select a movie and watch while having their MRI. In theory, this meant she did not have to be sedated for the procedure. As we had been told many times, sedation has its own set of risks that come along with any procedure. Little children in particular are at risk for over-sedation and can die if they receive too much sedation during any one procedure. We were blessed to have the ability for her to be without sedation during any one of her multiple MRI's. This particular feature of an MRI machine was not available in Fort Worth, so she either had to stay very still for over an hour, which is difficult for a four year old, or she had to be sedated. This was an unexpected blessing from God and it was only 30 miles from home.

We got into a room in the PICU and were scheduled for her MRI in the morning. We had stopped on the way so that she could eat because our experience had been that in any given situation, they may not let her eat for hours. We were safely there, hoping that someone there could give us the answers we were looking for.

The next morning, turned into the afternoon and we were finally brought in for her MRI. She picked her movie, SpongeBob, and for the next hour I would be by her side, holding her hand, listening to the knocking of the MRI machine. The machine was

79

so loud that I was given earplugs. Allie had her headphones on, while she listened to her movie, to help drown out the ridiculously loud banging of the gigantic machine that she was helplessly strapped into. She was amazing, as she had been since the first day of this nightmare. She literally could find the good, in almost every procedure she had. She looked forward to picking a movie and watching it during her MRI's. Her attitude throughout this entire nightmare was nothing less than God-like; smiling at those who were responsible for causing her so much discomfort and showing strength well beyond her years.

During the CT scan, which was a smaller, much quieter and quicker procedure than the MRI, she looked forward to the stickers and the bubbles that were given to her afterwards. As she was lying in bed, having to tolerate any number of IV's and blood draws, blood pressure and temperature checks, she looked forward to the meals. She would remove the lid from her plate with all the grace of a princess receiving breakfast in bed. And she loved having her mommy all to herself. Being the third of four, she didn't get this kind of one-on-one attention at home. Mommy's attention was clearly divided by four and she was enjoying every moment with me, and I was enjoying getting to spend that time with her. It was a gift, this experience, another gift from God. Sometimes God's gifts are wrapped in a way that we don't recognize them as such. Sometimes this gift felt like a "gag" gift, and other times a precious gift.

Being in Tulsa meant so much to us. Mom came by and brought Emma, my favorite breakfast burrito and Dr. Pepper from Sonic. Emma and Allie were so great together. I had missed seeing Emma so much and it was great to get to spend some time with her. The girls got to play in the playroom together and they had so much fun. Allie had to drag her IV pole with her everywhere she went but it didn't stop her. We had many visitors that day; several pastors from various churches visited and prayed with us. I loved that, it just made my day to have others asking God for strength and answers on our behalf. Granny and Pawpaw came up and brought the boys to see us. I missed my boys and my home; I missed everything about normal life. I decided that I would take advantage of the opportunity and take the kids home with me to spend the night in my bed at home. It had been weeks since I had done so. It was a horrible feeling, leaving Allie there with her daddy. I knew she was going to be fine, but I worried about leaving her and we had been through so much together. Of course, I didn't go home with the children until I had seen the doctor. That evening around 8:00, our pediatric neurologist came in to see us.

"She has had another stroke, this time a bad one that has damaged her right frontal lobe," the neurologist said. The bottom dropped out of my happy heart. He just kept shaking his head in disbelief. I had been right about how she was acting. I knew at that point that the over-dose had likely been at least a partial cause, but I also knew that this may have been a blessing in disguise. We were home where we needed to be and we were going to be taken care of. I hated that she had had yet another stroke, and not just another stroke, another bad stroke. And I hated that it meant more treatments, more uncertainty and more painful procedures for Allie. And then he said something that made me question his sanity. "I want you to go back down to Fort Worth, they know what to do about this sort of thing and I trust them to take good care of you. You will leave in the morning, and they will fly you using their emergency transport," he said. I began to cry. I was exhausted and didn't know if I could do it all again.

I looked to the heavens and tearfully said, "Okay, Lord, I need your help." What was looking like a light at the end of our tunnel was turning into another beginning to the nightmare. Although Allie seemed to be getting better after the strokes, she was having more of them, and that shook me to my core. I began to wonder if this was going to be our life now; if she was going to continue to deteriorate to the point that she would no longer be Allie. I wondered if we would continue to not have answers and things would just keep happening that were beyond our imagination, beyond our control. I had always found that through prayer, I could be at peace with whatever was happening at the time. And so, I began to pray for peace, strength, and answers. I prayed endlessly. Only God knew the answers, and only He knew when I would be ready to hear them. Tearfully, but with a smile on my face I took the children home, we made a pallet in the middle of the living room, picked a movie and went to sleep. I had the boys on either side of me, and Emma was lying on top of me. I was so happy. I felt so loved, so missed and so content. I still wasn't sleeping in my bed, but I was with my babies and I was happy. I had no idea how desperately I needed that respite until I was surrounded by my children, on my living room floor, in my own house for the night. Once again, we were blessed.

We love because he first loved us. 1 John 4:19

CHAPTER 12

⇾❁⇽

We woke and ate breakfast and dressed for the hospital. Donald would need to be relieved so that he could come home and dress for work. I gathered up some things I had been missing while in Texas to bring to the hospital this time. We arrived and prepared to be flown again to Fort Worth by emergency air transport. I went immediately to the gift shop and purchased my roll of antacids, my bottled water and was ready to go.

Upon arriving in Texas, Allie began having headaches. We were admitted to the PICU again and she was put on Heparin through her IV. They liked the Heparin because it was easy to discontinue should she need an emergency procedure or surgery. They put Allie on Morphine because she was in such pain with her headaches. They ran her down to the MRI to get a picture with and without contrast. I talked them into not sedating her based on her performance in Tulsa. She held still and strong for the MRI and the dye injection. Once again, she continually amazed me. What a blessing God had given me. Even though she was going through such trials, she was always smiling. She had such an even temperament and such strength. I used her strength and her smiles to pick me up when I was near my breaking points, and there were many.

But something began to change with Allie. The smiling and the even temperament were no longer a constant. They only held true in the daylight hours. At night she would wake up around 1:00 a.m. and scream her head off. It was almost as if, she was having some sort of night terror, or she would awaken with an excruciating headache.

She couldn't tell us what was wrong, she could only scream and cry. There was no way of determining exactly what the problem was. I felt amazingly helpless during those times. She would call to me, but if I tried to help her, she would kick and hit me and scream, as if in pain. I would stay back and give her some space; this only proved to make her even more upset. She would flail almost to the point of rolling herself out of bed and onto the floor. She would scream, not just a scream, but a wailing high pitched squeal that was likely only heard by dogs. We were hearing it in the openness of what I called the general population of seriously ill children, separated only by a curtain. She would wake everyone up; not only in the PICU, but on the entire second floor of the hospital. Her blood pressure would spike during these times and the hustling of the nursing staff would begin. They would ask me what she wanted or needed. I had no idea but the one thing I could assume was that she was in so much pain that she was inconsolable. I thought that maybe she was so over stimulated by a day filled with pokes and pulls and procedures, her only response to the enormously painful day was to scream like a crazy person for two hours in the middle of the night. Out of good ideas, I sat on the chair beside her and just threw my sheet over my head and plugged my ears with my fingers. I closed my eyes and prayed that God would rid Allie of this pain. It was then that they knew, they would have to give her Versed to sedate her. This was not just for her well-being, due to the fact that if her blood pressure spiked she was likely to have another stroke, but also because of the fact that there were critically ill children in the PICU of the hospital. Every night between one and two in the morning, she expressed herself this way. I told the nurses she was giving them her strongly worded letter of dissatisfaction with what has been going on with her. They laughed, but I thought that may be exactly what she was doing. She had limited communication skills and she was unable to accurately describe how she was feeling or ask for something that she needed. Most of the time, we just ended up sedating her, but sometimes, and those were the times I felt most useful, I could move her from her bed onto my lap where I could rock and sing her back to sleep. As she sobbed, I could feel her rapid heartbeat throughout her tiny body. I would hold her, hug her, kiss her head and pray to God that He would relieve her of this pain.

We met with the neurologists on Friday, June 13, 2008 and they gave us the news; news that would shock us. Allie's carotid arteries were completely blocked. There are only four main arteries that supply blood to the brain; Allie was down to two. She still had her vertebral arteries in the back that were supplying blood to her brain. However, the two vertebral arteries are not enough to supply the vast supply of blood and oxygen that the brain needs. Allie needed brain surgery. There were several options for her surgery, one was a procedure called a "burr-hole". They explained that the "burr-hole" procedure involved drilling holes in her skull cavity to allow the brain to send signals to the surrounding tissue to send blood. When this happens, arteries called collateral arteries would grow and help to supply blood to the brain. Collateral blood vessels are smaller and weaker and it takes many more of them to counteract the major artery dissections that had happened with Allie. Another option presented to us was patching a new membrane on top of her brain to help supply the brain with blood and oxygen. Again, this procedure would require collaterals to grow, a process that would require from three to six months before any type of difference would be seen. I began to cry again, and I immediately called on my prayer warriors for help. I typed into the "CarePages":

Please continue to keep us in your prayers at this time. She has been through so much, and I want her to keep her precious smile and good attitude. We are in need of a place to stay in Fort Worth as we could be here for a month or so and the Ronald McDonald house is full at present. Words cannot express how much we love you all and appreciate your prayers. Thank you all again for everything you have done for us.

Saturday, June 14th, we heard from the neurosurgeon. He explained that the plan was to have a repeat arteriogram, which is a procedure where a catheter is inserted through an artery in her leg and into her brain. Dye is then injected into the catheter and observed to see how it flows throughout the brain. This gives the doctors information about which arteries are carrying blood to the brain and what areas of the brain are not getting enough blood. He was sure to stress that even with the surgery, it would take between three and six months before we saw any type of improvement in her symptoms. Her arteriogram was scheduled for Monday and her brain surgery would be scheduled either Wednesday or Thursday of that week. They wouldn't know what surgery was a possibility until after her arteriogram on Monday. Uncertainty was no stranger to us.

On Sunday morning, Allie was uncharacteristically fussy. They had to put an arterial line on her right hand because the blood quit drawing out of her neck. She was still on the Heparin because it was easy to stop for the arteriogram and neurosurgery. Allie had a beautiful head of blonde hair that was a complete mess. Her head was very tender from having the strokes and she did not tolerate anyone combing it without a handful of conditioner. Because she had lines in her neck and in her hands, she wasn't able to take a bath or a shower. Some of the nurses said that there was a beautician that volunteered at the hospital one day a week who could cut Allie's hair shorter so that it didn't get so many tangles in it. They gave the beautician a call and Allie was on the books for a cut at 1:00 on Sunday afternoon. We were so excited, just for a change of pace that day. We both loved having something to look forward to. Days in the hospital went slowly and could be very lonely. Time was measured by each procedure, each poke, each meal, each pill or medication change. Monotonous at best, the hours dragged and it became very difficult to keep busy. The weekends were the worst. There were fewer staff and volunteers, and the hours at the gift shop and the coffee shop were shortened. Sunday's beautician's visit was a blessing, something different, something to look forward to. Sunday at 1:00 p.m. came and went without a change. We found out later that she had gotten busy with something else and was unable to come; disappointment again.

This particular Sunday was also Father's Day and Donald was at home with everyone else. It was already a depressing day with the beautician standing us up. Allie was sad and I was doing my best to lift both of our spirits, but it was a losing battle. Then as always, God stepped in and provided us with a blessing and a smile. A prayer was answered as the Ronald McDonald house called and said they had a room for us. My eyes swelled with tears as my heart swelled with love and appreciation for our gracious God. This meant a place for mom to stay and a place for the kids to stay when they visited. We were thrilled, and soon after, Allie was able to record a video for her daddy.

She said "Happy Father's Day Daddy" and then she smiled. I e-mailed it to him right away. It made his day and mine.

> *Be strong and courageous. Do not fear or be in dread of them, for it is the LORD your God who goes with you. He will not leave you or forsake you. Deuteronomy 31:6*

Monday, June 16th, was very busy as most weekdays had become in the hospital world. Preparations had to be made for the significant 48 hours to come. Allie's arteriogram had been re-scheduled for 12:00 p.m. on Tuesday and was supposed to take between one and two hours. She would have to be sedated for this one; there wasn't any getting around it. The neurosurgeon did mention that it was not likely that he would do a bypass procedure on her. He stated that there were only about two neurosurgeons in the country that could do that procedure on such a small child. At the time, I didn't think to ask him who or where. He said the burr-hole procedure was the safest and least invasive procedure to do on her. He stated that he would be drilling four holes in her head on each side toward the top and back so as not to interfere with the collaterals that had already been forming in the frontal region of her brain. The Physical Therapist visited Allie and they had a blast playing and walking around. The Child Life Specialist at the hospital brought Allie her own special doll. I helped Allie color it, as she wasn't able to do this herself just yet. The CLS also gave Allie things to play doctor with her special doll. Allie was able to put a wristband on her doll and she even got to put an IV in her dolls neck. Allie loved taking a syringe full of water and injecting it into the dolls IV port on her neck. I gave Allie a pedicure that evening, we washed her hair very carefully and I braided it for her. It was a very precious time for us to be able to spend time alone. Time spent in the hospitals didn't afford us much alone and interrupted time. She loved it almost as much as I did.

Tuesday, June 17th, was all about getting Allie prepped for her arteriogram procedure. The procedure began before noon and lasted until 3 p.m. that afternoon. During those times, I would take advantage of the alone time to regain some sanity or eat a meal at a table with silverware and napkins. The hospital had television screens that showed serene scenes of waterfalls and birds singing. I loved to get a soda and just sit and watch the screens. I loved even more going outside and just walking around, enjoying the fresh air. I didn't dare go too far though. There was a phone in the waiting area that was used to alert waiting family members that a patient was finished with a procedure. I couldn't imagine missing that call. And so, my respite was short lived as I returned to wait nervously with my mom for that phone that to ring. When it was finally our call, I was both relieved and scared. The interventional radiologist met with us to say that she had already developed some collateral vessels. This was good news he explained; it was the body's way of repairing itself which was considerably easier than having another human go in and mess with things. But once again, it was a small victory that was short lived. The collaterals were smaller and weaker and she just was not getting enough blood flow to her brain. He was going to discuss it with the neurosurgeon and the neurosurgeon would be getting with us.

I was getting little, if any sleep, at night and none during the day. Allie continued to have her screaming fits that would begin anywhere from 1 a.m. to 3 a.m. Allie wouldn't let me out of her sight and so I was primarily sleeping in the chair beside her. I was also on the every-other-day plan for a shower at the Ronald McDonald house. My mom had driven down and was staying there so that we could keep the room. Mom would come up to the hospital and sit with Allie while I walked to the Ronald McDonald house to get a shower. A shower was one of the things that helped me feel human again. I would have loved to have slept in the room, in a bed, but Allie would have no part of it. Allie's fits were bad when I was there; I cannot imagine how bad the fits would have been had I not been there.

During those times, I don't know what I would have done without my mother. She brought me my bagel and cream cheese in the morning along with my iced tea and exactly ten packets of sugar. Food was not officially allowed in the PICU, but the nurses allowed it because it didn't have a strong smell and because they did not want Allie's blood pressure to go up with her fits. Every fit caused her blood pressure to spike to 210/160 and she would have to be given a sedative in order to calm down. Allie loved my mother. She would even tolerate staying with my mother on the rare opportunities I had to get lunch or dinner, or just take a walk. My mother was an answer to prayer as well. Allie was in God's hands and had been since before she was born. He was also looking out for me and had put people in my life at strategic times and in strategic places that were helping me. People we didn't even know were praying for us, sending us money and sending Allie care packages. We were blessed beyond measure.

On Thursday June 19th, Allie had her first brain surgery at Cook Children's Hospital in Fort Worth, Texas. As difficult and stressful as things had been leading up to this day, I had an enormous sense of peace fall over me during her surgery. The fear and uncertainty that I had lived with for so many weeks was gone. I knew beyond a doubt that God was watching over her. God was taking care of her; He was guiding the neurosurgeon's hands. He was in control. He is a good and loving God, and He especially loves His little children.

He only is my Rock and my Salvation; He is my Defense and my Fortress, I shall not be moved. Psalm 62:6

Allie made it through surgery and was in recovery. She was very sleepy and swollen, especially on her left side, but conscious. The doctor was only able to make one oblong hole directly above her ear on each side. The muscle was too thin everywhere else. That was it; that was all he felt comfortable doing with her and it would just have to be enough. They were careful to wash all the blood out of her hair before they brought her down to us. She looked like an angel. I gently grabbed her hand and I didn't let go. I finally ended up beside her in bed, snuggling with her until she fell asleep. I was again, truly amazed by her strength. Morphine and exhaustion helped her sleep through the night for the first time in weeks.

Allie woke up the next morning and she was really swollen. She said it hurt to open her mouth, to chew and to swallow. I could see and feel the sutures where they had drilled the holes on either side of her head. It would be a while before we would be able to comb her hair again. We would not be able to wash her hair until her sutures were dissolved and her head would be very sore for a while. The neurologist had sent her images to a stroke specialist in Houston, to confirm that her arteries had dissected. A dissected artery is very rare for a four year old. Those types of arteries are reserved for the elderly, or those with extremely high cholesterol.

Allie slept in the next day but woke up twice during the evening asking for chocolate milk. She was supposed to be drinking fluids like water or juice. Because she had been in bed for weeks, as well as all of the pain killers and anesthesia, she was constipated. She had gone nine days without a bowel movement and the nurses were beginning to get concerned. The nurses, especially in the PICU measured everything. They wanted to know how much she ate of everything, how much fluid she had taken and how much she had eliminated. After everything else she had been through, Allie was given a suppository, to get things going. She had been taking a mild laxative just to keep things moving, but it wasn't helping her very much. Needless to say, after the suppository and the following bathroom break, she was feeling much better. The PICU nurses were all relieved as well. Allie did not drink a lot of fluids normally, except for chocolate milk. She would drink throughout the day at home, but not near enough for the standards in the PICU. She was held to a higher standard of performance in the hospital than she was at home.

Bad news again; the doctors in Houston agreed that her arteries had indeed dissected. They, along with everyone else, still had no idea why this had happened to Allie. It was not for a lack of trying. They had literally run every test they could think of and had come up with absolutely no answers except that she was normal in every way. Test results could not explain or deny the fact that her arteries had been dissecting for years and she had suffered several strokes, including the two most recent which were significant. It was more than discouraging. Allie had been put through more physical and emotional distress at four years old than most of us endure in our whole lives; all of this and still no results. But I knew that God would keep us in His loving hands so I never gave up hope.

Rejoice in hope, be patient in tribulation, be constant in prayer.
Romans 12:12

CHAPTER 13

—❧❀❧—

Allie was out of surgery and so far the results were good. Things seemed to be settling down and shifting in our favor for a change. We were ready to go to the floor and get ourselves into a regular room with a shower and bathtub so that she could take a bath. Donald had come to Texas for her surgery and had brought the kids with him. It was wonderful to see them all but their visits seemed to always end with a similar result. As usual, Emma had thrown a fit because she did not want to leave Allie and me, so we allowed her to stay with my mother, at the Ronald McDonald house. This seemed to be agreeable to Emma. However, Emma was a four year old with moods as unpredictable as the Oklahoma weather. My mother had taken Emma from our room after saying our goodbyes at the hospital. She got all the way to the Ronald McDonald house and began preparing Emma for bed. Emma began to miss her mommy and this is where the unpredictability began. Emma began rocking, moaning and screaming and my mother was certain that they were going to be thrown out of the Ronald McDonald House. Emma began what my mother termed as her own personal "Trail of Tears". She dragged Emma back to the hospital, stopping every few steps to attempt a soothing grandmother embrace. By the time they made it to the hospital, my mother was dripping wet from sweat. Emma was inconsolable and unreasonable considering they were heading back to see us. My mother had to stop to pry her hands off of the benches and railings throughout the hospital as they made their way. They barely made it to the security desk where they were able to go no further because it was after visiting hours. I left Allie's room in the PICU at 10:00 p.m. to retrieve my exhausted visitors from the security station. As I arrived, I noticed my mother looked exhausted and Emma's eyes were swollen from crying. Her skin was mottled red and white from the stress of her adventure and I wasn't sure exactly what I was going to do at this point. I proposed that my mom would stay with Allie for the night and I would take Emma to the Ronald McDonald House and stay with her. Mom went to Allie's room and I proceeded to walk with Emma back to the house. She clung to me tightly the entire evening. She woke several times crying and flailing, until she could feel my body next to hers and then she would calm. She would take my hand, hold it and nestle in closely while she fell back to sleep. I was able to sleep that night, only because I was certain that Allie was fine in the PICU with mother. If I had only known the truth of what was transpiring with Allie, I am not sure what I would have done.

We arrived back at the hospital that morning and my mother gave the report of what had transpired that night at the hospital. Apparently, Allie was displeased with my idea of having my mother stay with her in the room and so made herself known to everyone that evening. She threw the fit that rocked the hospital that evening and again had to be sedated with Versed. I felt completely defeated. I could not physically be in two places at the same time; however that was exactly what I needed to do. I called my husband at home in Oklahoma and told him that Emma's being here was not working out. She was unable to stay without me and I was unable to keep her in the PICU overnight as it was against hospital policy. Donald said that he would not be able to come back up and get her until Monday. I was uncertain as to what to do. I gave it to God to show me the answer.

That evening, we decided to keep both girls happy and just hang out in the room together. The nurse came in from time to time and noticed Emma but never said anything. Around midnight, the nurse asked if Emma was staying there this evening. I explained that she was and that we didn't really have a choice about it. She said it wasn't allowed and that we would need to go back to the Ronald McDonald House or stay in the waiting room with her through the night. My mom and I explained the impossible situation we were having. We explained that if I had left with Emma, Allie would have a fit so dramatic that she would need sedation and that if I stayed with Allie and mother took Emma, Emma would throw a fit so mighty that they may actually be thrown out of the Ronald McDonald House. After much debate about the legalities of the situation, I asked if there was a form I could fill out that would relieve them of any responsibility if Emma got hurt during the night. They reluctantly agreed and all was well for the evening. Emma and I slept on the chair right next to Allie's bed and all were happy, for now.

The next day, they ridded themselves of us in the PICU. We were finally on a floor and Emma could stay with us in the room for as long as we did. Being on a floor was much more like regular life than the PICU. Everyone on the floor was so much more relaxed about measuring things. They only checked on us every couple of hours or so and we were allowed to leave and go anywhere on the grounds of the hospital, inside or outside of the hospital. Allie immediately got a bath and we were given permission to wash her hair lightly without scrubbing. It took me 45 minutes, but I was able to comb the rats out of her hair. She looked precious. She had been set free and she looked great. She was running all over the floor with Emma. I had to run to keep up with them in case Allie fell. We all went downstairs and got to meet a "Princess", we also ran into "Chuck-E-Cheese" downstairs and he gave her a stuffed mouse to take home. We went up to the fourth floor and were able to join a summer camp in progress where we got to paint and color. Allie and Emma were having a blast. She was so much happier on the floor and she looked so good. Then another answered prayer; the neurologist came in and told us we were going home on aspirin therapy. She was to take one a day for the rest of her life. He also went through the risks associated with her ever being able to take birth control pills, skydive, or scuba dive and she was to stay away from roller coasters. Apparently, drop in blood pressures could result in TIA (Transient Ischemic Attack—mini-stroke) activity or another stroke. Before we left, they took us into a room and gave us "the talk". They wanted to be certain that we understood the seriousness of her condition. She was at risk for seizures; great risk. She was also at great risk for another stroke. The stroke that she was at great risk for could kill her or would, at best, leave her in such a state that she would no longer be recognizable to us. They had no answers for us as to what had caused her condition which they were now referring to as Moyamoya, a condition of tangled arteries blocking blood flow to the brain. One of her neurologist actually had tears in his eyes as he spoke, "She is just so precious, she keeps me awake at night because I feel helpless to help her." We were discharged for home with an enormous amount of uncertainty about what lay ahead. We had great faith though, great faith that God had taken good care of her for a reason, and that her journey was not over yet. He was not finished with her yet.

> *Trust in the Lord and do good; so you will live in the land, and enjoy security. Take delight in the Lord and he will give you the desires of your heart. Commit your way to the Lord; trust in him, and he will act. Be still before the Lord, and wait patiently for him. Psalm 37:3-5, 7a*

We made the trip home and we were welcomed home by everyone. My friends and family called, asked about her and wanted to come by and see her. Each one that came by looked at her in almost disbelief. She looked like a normal little girl. Aside from some balance problems and her right arm (which for the most part was hanging at her side), she looked great. If she was running at all, she would pull that hand and wrist up almost in a protective way as not to hit it on anything. If she was asked a question, it would take her a while to answer it, but she still had her perfect smile. Life was back to normal for all of us. God had brought my baby girl back.

> *Those who love me, I will deliver; I will protect those who know my name. When they call to me, I will answer them; I will be with them in trouble, I will rescue them and honor them. With long life I will satisfy them, and show them my salvation. Psalm 91: 14-16*

On vacation before the massive stroke in May of 2008.

In the motor home before the 3rd surgery.

All four before the stroke. Adam, Allie Brennan and Emma.

Brennan and Adam posing by Adam's legos.

Allie's makeover after her Burr Holes.

At inpatient rehab having a visit with Emma.

Allie loves to swim in the hot tub.
Perfect. This was before her brain
angiogram in Fort Worth.

Allie after 2nd surgery in Stanford California.

Half Moon Bay after 4th surgery.

The girls in their soccer uniforms.

CHAPTER 14

❧ ✿ ❧

The girls were both ready to go to Pre-K. We enrolled them at the school where I was working as a Kindergarten Teacher. This was again, part of God's plan. At no time during the course of my education, did I plan to be a teacher. I had a Bachelor's degree in Psychology from the University of Tulsa and a Master's degree from Oklahoma State University in Child Development. None of those degrees allowed me a certification in education. I had gone the route of the Alternative Certification. For a time, in Oklahoma, if you had a degree in something relevant, you were allowed to become certified in that area through a series of recommendations, interviews and completed tests. I was initially certified as a home economics teacher for grades sixth to twelfth. I was eventually allowed to become certified in early childhood. Before any of this happened with Allie, I was getting most of the children with special needs in my classroom. Therefore, I decided to become certified in special education. I've heard that the Lord doesn't call those who are prepared but He prepares those who are called. It was His plan that I had all the training for children with special needs and was raising four children that all had special needs as well as one in particular that was medically fragile. I enrolled the girls in school, feeling completely at peace because I would be there with them, just a couple of rooms down, teaching kindergarten. God knew what we needed, even years before we needed it.

So do not be like them; for your Father knows what you need before you ask Him. Matthew 6:8

Allie loved school but it was difficult for her to get up in the morning. She was having TIA's or mini-strokes often because she was awakened too early and she hadn't had enough sleep. Allie required much sleep and I made it a priority that year. I wanted her brain to have the best chance it could to restore the blood supply itself and sleep was its best asset. I made the decision to move Allie and Emma to the afternoon pre-k rather than the morning pre-k to give her a couple of hours more to sleep. Her daddy was on the evening shift and didn't leave for work until 2:30, so he was easily able to drop the girls off at school early in the afternoon. This also gave us an opportunity for Allie to get therapy at Summit. Summit was an amazing place that offered outpatient rehab for children and was only a couple of miles from our house. They took our insurance and we couldn't have been more pleased that Allie's therapy was only going to be about $120 each week. She would get Occupational Therapy twice a week, Physical Therapy once a week and Speech Therapy once a week. In school, she was getting speech therapy once a week, physical therapy twice a month and occupational therapy once a week. In addition to all of the formal therapies, she was constantly trying to keep up with her sister and her two older brothers. There wasn't anything she would let them beat her at and that in itself was therapy for her. She had to relearn everything in the way of eating, writing, coloring, painting, and cutting in school using her left hand. She was doing amazingly well. Once we made the decision to move them to the afternoon class, she began to do incredibly well. Allie seemed to know when she was going to have a TIA; it was usually after she had been crying a lot and it happened when her blood pressure would get low. She seemed to understand that and would lie down somewhere so she wouldn't fall down and hurt herself. Often, she would lose the ability to speak. She would just look at me and I would know she was in the middle of what we called an "episode". The episodes could last anywhere from five minutes to a couple of hours. We were instructed just to watch and time them, and note which areas were involved. I could handle the five minute TIA's but I started to get very nervous if they lasted much longer than that. I never knew if she was going to have another full stroke. I never knew if this would be the one that would take our little girl from us forever.

Allie was having TIA's anywhere from one to three times a week. No matter what we did, we could not stop her day to day aggravation of living in a house with two older brothers. They loved her very much, but they did not give her any special privileges. If she messed with their things, they immediately grabbed them out of her hands, or they sang at the top of their lungs to what she decided was "her" songs. All the same activity as any other family, only a fit thrown by Allie would result in a TIA that could leave her lifeless and unable to speak for anywhere from five minutes to an hour.

Slowly our family began to move back into normalcy. The normal fights, the normal laughter, the normal schedules and the normal challenges for all of the kids. That particular year was a revelation in the life of our oldest son Brennan. Brennan was in the fifth grade and he was having a very difficult time in school. I had gone part-time, in order to better meet Allie's needs and all of her doctor appointments. Surprisingly, I found myself spending a great deal of my time at the South Campus of Brennan's school. I had multiple meetings with his teacher, all summing up the same problems. He wasn't turning in his homework, he was losing his papers, and he was disorganized and easily distracted. I told his teacher the problems I was having at home, helping him with his homework; how we would literally sit for more than three hours at the dining room table and torture ourselves while attempting to finish the homework that he was unable to finish in class. He was distracted by everything within a five-mile radius of that kitchen table. We would turn the television off and ban the other children to their rooms. He would lie down on the dining room chairs, completely exasperated and unable to find a starting place, much less a finishing place on his homework. I was completely frustrated; I did not have three hours every night to do nothing but sit at a dining room table and help my oldest son with his homework. It wasn't that he didn't deserve my time with him; to the contrary, I felt enormous guilt for spending the last several months completely engulfed in all of his sister's medical problems. I went to a local office supply store and began the quest to help my son organize himself and his workspace at school. I went to his school and started with his locker. I got him some magnetic shelves and things to organize his locker to help him better get his papers to class. I then got him some colored binders to organize his subjects to also better help him get his things turned in. He had a ridiculous amount of zeros in the grade book all from papers he couldn't find. Then, I attacked his desk. I was amazed at the things I found shoved up against the back of his desk. Papers that he was supposed to have turned in, but didn't. I found unsharpened pencils that had been chewed into unrecognizable shapes and erasers that had also been chewed on so that they no longer were able to fulfill their original function. I organized his desk and began to look around the room. I didn't see any other mothers in there organizing and painstakingly rummaging through their child's desk. I asked his teacher, "Is this normal?"

I was almost relieved when she said, "Actually no. Brennan has a degree of distractibility and disorganization that goes beyond the typical fifth grader." I had another precious child who apparently exceeded the norm, where dysfunctional behaviors were concerned. We decided that we needed to do some assessments of Brennan's behaviors and so we consulted a developmental pediatrician. We loved her at once. She completely connected with Brennan and they had a great rapport from the very beginning. She gave us all of the home and classroom inventories and his fifth grade teacher and I filled everything out on Brennan. We took everything back to our developmental pediatrician and she diagnosed him with Attention Deficit Disorder with Hyperactivity. She put him on Vyvannse and we were able to add another blessing to our pile of blessings that God had given us. The Vyvannse worked perfectly for him. It had only one side effect, it took his appetite away while he was on it during the day. By 8:00 p.m. he was rummaging through the cabinets like a crazy man eating everything in sight and leaving an unprecedented mess in the kitchen. But, during the day, he was completely focused, turning in assignments and miraculously never had homework again. He was able to get everything done at school. He finished any homework that was assigned as soon as he got off the bus, before I got home from school. It was amazing. With Brennan having growth problems and thyroid problems, not eating was a big problem. Every time we visited the endocrinologist, she would plead with Brennan to eat lunch even if he wasn't hungry, and to take his thyroid medicine, even when he didn't take his Vyvannse on the weekends. Personally, I was not a fan of medication for ADHD before my child was diagnosed with it. I believe that positive behaviors can be taught and negative behaviors can be extinguished. But nothing convinced me that my son had a chemical imbalance in his brain more than the effects I saw when he was on the medication. He was cooperative, agreeable, alert, focused, kind, organized and willing to help around the house when he was on his medication. Without his medication, which we experience on weekends, holidays and in the summer, he was argumentative, slovenly, angry, forgetful, inattentive, and unpleasant most of the time to say the least. In fact, he refused to go to school if he forgot to take his medicine. He felt better about himself, went from B's to A's within a year and his ability to organize his own space and work was dramatically improved. I was aware however, that there are children who go through any number of medications and spend years trying to get it right where their disability is concerned. We tried one medication and it worked like a dream. God's work in our lives continued to amaze me.

Toward the end of the school year in May of 2009, the girls debuted for the first time on stage at the Justus-Tiawah school Talent Show. They sang a very short, acapella song that they had memorized from one of their favorite movies. They sang it using a microphone in front of no less than 500 people. They were a huge hit and I was so proud of them. They had come so far since their premature birth, and Allie had really shown progress during the year. It was hard to believe that it had only been a year since she had her strokes and we had done the hospital tour of the continental Midwest. It was hard to even let my mind go back there. It was a time that I would love to have forgotten, except that I could see it in my little girl every time I looked at her. It was always there; her right arm and hand, "righty" we called it, lifeless by her side or drawn up near her shoulder when she ran. The evidence was far too clear every time I looked at her. Why couldn't I just see how far she had come? Why couldn't I ignore the wrapping and just see the gift? Why did I have to focus on the little parts of her that were no longer working properly? I know it had everything to do with the fact that there was her identical twin, behind her developmentally at one time, now passing her before our very eyes. Although, she was able to write her name and color with her left hand, she had to relearn that and it wasn't as refined as her sister's was. Allie would notice it sometimes and so would Emma. Emma would say, "Allie's the baby now, right momma?" I ached for my baby girl that had to relearn everything. She used to be the one who could keep time with the music and had an amazing little singing voice for a four year old, and now, it came slower, not as in tune as it once was. She was also very nasal sounding in her speaking voice. It was as if, every muscle on the right side of her body, including her larynx had been affected. My twins who were once identical in every way were now easily distinguished.

Allie had been receiving therapy at an outpatient pediatric facility and she had been receiving what they referred to as "co-treats". In general, they were promoted to us as child friendly and more appropriate for children Allie's age. They involved one hour sessions with two therapists; an Occupational Therapist and a Physical therapist would work with Allie at the same time. This sounded great at first, not that it diminished our copayments at all, it was still $30 per therapist per hour and they were both billing our insurance company for the full hour regardless of how many of them worked together with Allie. This began another of our challenges.

The facility was billing each discipline identically for the same hour on the same day of service. This presented numerous problems. With the same billing code being sent twice for the same hour on the same day, the insurance company was denying one of them because they assumed one service was double billed. It was easy for me to understand, I wasn't sure why the facility didn't understand the insurance company's reasoning. In January of 2009, the facility's customer service called me into a special room at Allie's therapy visit and explained that my insurance was not paying for the co-treatments in a timely manner and that they would like for me to contact my insurance company and convince them to pay the co-treatments as they are billed. I was not an advocate for our insurance company but they have never refused any services that Allie needed and paid for treatments outside of our home state as well as each and every one of the flights that Allie took from Tulsa to Fort Worth with no questions whatsoever. So, when I was taken aside and told that my insurance company wasn't paying a mere $76 for treatment per week, I found that difficult to believe. They had easily paid more than half a million dollars for her treatments. Being agreeable, and not wanting to argue about it, I immediately told the facility to discontinue all co-treatments since they were not being paid. We didn't have the kind of money they wanted. If the insurance company didn't pay, we would be responsible for the entire amount, not just the contracted amount. I went straight home and contacted our insurance company. They explained the billing situation and asked me to have the facility bill them under a different code if it was a different service; they were even nice enough to give me a couple of codes that they could choose from and they would pay it. I immediately contacted the billing representative at the facility with the information from the insurance company. She told me that she would be committing insurance fraud if she billed it that way and that what they were asking her to do was a crime. I knew nothing about insurance, billing or codes but I knew that my daughter would need therapy for possibly the rest of her life. I also knew that there were no other pediatric therapy facilities in our area so I continued to be in the middle of what would continue to be an ongoing battle between the rehab facility and our insurance company. I made all of the phone calls, brought in all the information the insurance company sent to me and left the rest to the "professionals." I continued to pay my co-payments as they were billed to me but in early May of 2009, a day before a scheduled session, the clinic director called to tell me that our account was still outstanding and they could no longer treat Allie. I was a mess. Allie had to have therapy, she couldn't miss. I cried and began to pray, "Lord, give me peace where I feel anger, give me help to find a place for Allie that can work with our insurance company. Please let the insurance company just pay the facility, we don't have the money to pay for it out of pocket." I was being very specific in this prayer. Through God's grace, the facility had actually called while we were on our way to the girls' pediatrician. When the doctor appeared she knew something was wrong; not with either girl this time. I began to cry and told the doctor what was happening. She said, "If they want me to call them and tell them how to bill it I will. What can I do to help you?" She told us that the local hospital now had outpatient rehab and she was certain they had an Occupation therapist on staff. We could get speech services from another local rehab facility and so, I made the call. God again, answered our prayers.

The local hospital had an amazing, caring and precious Occupational Therapist that absolutely loved Allie. Allie loved Miss Connie and Miss Connie loved Allie; it was a match made in heaven.

We had two things we had never had at the other place, the insurance was paying without any problems, and she stayed with Miss Connie for almost a year. At the other rehab facility, it seemed like Allie got a new therapist every month or so. This made it very difficult for Allie, always having to get acquainted with a new therapist. Old debts were paid and Allie finally loved therapy. I knew God had answered our prayers once again.

> *Ask and it will be given to you; seek and you will find; knock and the door will be opened to you. For everyone who asks receives; he who seeks finds; and to him who knocks, the door will be opened. Matthew 7:7–8*

CHAPTER 15

—⇾❀⇽—

After school was out in May of 2009, I had a hysterectomy. I had been putting it off for obvious reasons, but I felt good about how Allie was doing. I felt like we were finally at a point of stability. But as so many small victories before, this too would be short lived. While I was recuperating in the hospital, Allie took a turn for the worse. She had been playing outside, following Donald around and suddenly she said, "Daddy my arms feel heavy." Donald turned around just in time to see her fall to the ground, lifeless. He picked her up and rushed her into the house where he could see she was still breathing. He called me at the hospital to tell me what had happened. Allie had gone without any TIA's for a while, but these episodes had become such a part of our lives that familiarity had replaced shock. However, this one was different. This particular episode had not followed a screaming, crying fit like others. Allie recovered as she had with each of the previous episodes. We noted it, but kept going with life as usual. After leaving the hospital, I stayed at my mother's house and she cared for me while I still had a catheter in. The day after I arrived at my mom's, Allie fell to the ground again with the exact same symptoms. This time, I called the doctors in Fort Worth. The doctors knew that Allie was at extreme risk of seizures from her brain damage and so they wanted to see her immediately. I was totally helpless. I had just undergone major surgery and was unable to sit up, much less endure a six hour road trip and take care of a child who was possibly seizing to the point that she could drop to the ground lifeless. I wasn't supposed to pick anything up heavier than my shoe for the next month so I sat this one out. My husband drove her to Fort Worth, checked them into a hospital and drove them to the emergency room where they were immediately seen by the hematologist and neurologist. They did another MRI/MRA of her brain and saw there was no new stroke activity. This was great news. They could not rule out seizure activity at this point, but they were fairly certain they were just TIA's. The doctors in Fort Worth decided to go with a more aggressive anticoagulant or blood thinner so they started Allie on Lovenox. Donald was visited by a home health nurse at the hotel and was shown how to give Allie the injections again, before returning home. She would have to be on Lovenox for a week before she could be switched to Coumadin. Allie would once again have to endure getting shots in her stomach; she was not happy. I came home to be there when they returned from Texas. She came home on the injections and after I was feeling a little better, I even gave her the injections when Donald was at work. I didn't like giving them to her. She wouldn't sit still for them and afterwards I would hold and rock her until she calmed down and we both felt better. The Coumadin was started and the Lovenox was discontinued. Coumadin levels had to be monitored closely. In addition to everything else that was going on, we had to take her to the hospital in Tulsa to have her blood drawn once or twice a week. Allie really hated those trips, as did I. Our summer was full of weekly trips to the hospital for blood draws, waiting for the Hematologist to call with instructions to adjust her Coumadin dose.

Summer soon gave way to fall and school began. Brennan was now in sixth grade and Adam was in second grade. Brennan was having a great start to his year and he was doing really well. Adam was also having a good year and his reading skills really took off. Adam was starting to really get noticed for his quirky behavior. He would talk to himself or say things at lunch that were off color and would generally get in trouble for it. He really didn't understand that telling the PE teacher "this sucks" was out of line. To Adam's defense he was apraxic, meaning he didn't know where his body was in space and the PE teacher's idea of fun was jump rope. For Adam, it did suck. He loved PE, running around, playing tag and different games but not jump rope. I tried to explain to his PE teacher that he was apraxic but my explanation fell on deaf ears. I apologized for Adam's rudeness and told him I would have a serious talk with

Adam about things he should not say at school. The other problem that really began to bother his teacher and his peers was Adam's inability to change his clothing from day to day. Shoes became an enormous issue as Adam refused to wear socks because the seam at the end bothered him. Wearing shoes without socks for weeks at a time in Oklahoma during August heat and humidity caused those shoes to create an aroma that can't be described with words, it had to be experienced. Unfortunately, Adam's shoe developed a hole out of which the terrible smell was escaping into his classroom, over his unsuspecting classmates. Because I was already there, it was easy to summon me from my classroom to help resolve the issues that came up with any one of my four children. Fortunately or unfortunately, teachers and principals always knew where to find me. And so, Adam's principal visited my room that day. She said that Adam had a smell around him and they wondered if I could check him and see where the smell is coming from. She also asked me if I could take him home and take care of the problem. I met with Adam in the office bathroom. He explained to me that his shoe had a hole in it. I explained to him that his dad was coming to get him to give him a bath and take him to buy new shoes. Socks were still an issue for Adam until finally I pleaded with him one day to not put either one of us through that again. He agreed. From that point on, he was wearing socks on a daily basis. Another small victory and blessing from God. I was so proud of him.

We enrolled the girls in kindergarten with my good friend Dawna Watkins. Dawna had not been without drama herself as she was the mother of triplets, two of which were boys and friends with Brennan. During that same summer, Dawna was in a near fatal car accident that caused her to be hospitalized with severe injuries. While she was hospitalized, I invited her children stay over at our house for a few days. Dawna recovered and began coming over to the house to visit with the girls. She knew they would be in her class in the fall and she wanted to be certain that they felt comfortable with her. She didn't want them to lose any time in their learning because they weren't feeling comfortable with her. She was amazing. She came to love my little girls and is still one of my dearest friends to this day. They began the school year with Mrs. Watkins as their kindergarten teacher. That year began all day school for the twins and Allie would always be exhausted by 2:00 p.m. I was grateful for Dawna; she knew Allie's medical history and watched her like a hawk. If she knew Allie was getting tired, she would let her lie down for some much needed rest in the reading center. If she thought Allie was sick, she would send her to me immediately. I was directly across the hall teaching Kindergarten so it was a perfect set up.

In October, Allie was receiving Physical and Occupational Therapy in school. One afternoon, our principal came to my room and said, "Something is wrong with Allie. She is in the office and she doesn't look good." They asked someone to cover my room and I went immediately to the office. I saw Allie lying on her Physical Therapists lap. As I tried to gain my composure, they began to tell me what had happened. Allie was coming through a play tunnel and had had an episode. She had fallen to the floor and wasn't able to speak. They carried her to the office to check her and immediately came to get me. However, they had left out a key piece to the story that I didn't find out until later. I took her home and watched her that evening. Allie had another one that night. Her eyes started to wander around in her head and she couldn't focus on me; it scared me. The doctors said to let them know if the episodes lasted more than thirty minutes or if there was a different part of her body involved. They thought she might be having another stroke if it involved another part of her body. I immediately called the neurologist in Fort Worth, explained the symptoms and my concerns. His only response was to ask, "How fast can you get down here?"

The drive to Fort Worth was never less than five hours and that is if I am doing a little more than the speed limit. I called my mom; we both packed a bag and were off. I called my husband from the road and told him we were on our way to Texas. He was shocked. I told him what had been going on with Allie but he was frustrated. By this point, he couldn't imagine what they could possibly do for her and he knew that with me and Allie gone, he would have to figure out how he would get the kids to school and watch them after school. It was nerve-racking to say the least. I was frustrated and felt unsupported. I hung up the phone and began to pray. I prayed that God would again give me strength to make good decisions for Allie. I asked for the strength to get through, whatever we were getting ready to go through and to give Donald the ability to understand what we are going through. It wasn't the first time I had felt unsupported by my spouse. He didn't handle stress very well and lately we had certainly seen our share. His coping mechanism was to deny that anything was wrong at first and then decide that everything was going to be fine. I envied that ability sometimes. I knew that at least one of us had to be prepared in case everything wasn't fine. I had a feeling that this time was going to be different; that this time everything wasn't going to be fine.

We drove to Fort Worth and went straight to the Emergency Room. They immediately checked us in and got us to the neurology floor. The neurologist wanted to hook her up to a continuous EEG machine to check for the possibility of seizure activity. She was at very high risk of having a seizure, although to date, the tests they had run were all negative for seizure activity. She would be on 72 hours of continuous EEG and video monitoring. She could be off the video monitoring for small period of time, but would take a portable EEG machine with her wherever she went. Normally, they would try to evoke an episode through various methods, strobe lights or blowing on a windmill toy, but the Seizure specialist did not want to be responsible for evoking a TIA and so he specifically told us not to try to evoke an episode. We would just sit and wait for one to happen.

Cook Children's Hospital at Fort Worth had enormous support from the community. They had activities that went on throughout the week and especially on the weekends. Of course, we were there over Halloween and they had a little "trick or treat" in the common area for all the children who were stuck in the hospital during Halloween. They asked Allie what she wanted to be for Halloween and through her beautiful smile she said a princess. They returned later that day with a beautiful princess dress exactly her size. She was precious. Her scalp was covered with wires but she still had that smile. The wires were about a foot and a half long and went from her head down into her portable EEG machine that she carried like a "fanny pack" on her hip. The wires were surrounded by gauze that covered everything except the very top of her head, where both her hair and the tangled mess of wires merged. That mess combined with her beautiful princess dress and her Cinderella candy bucket was truly a sight to behold. We made the circle throughout the foyer of all of the departments in the hospital who were donating their time and their trinket toys to the "trick-or-treat" for children who were stuck at the hospital on Halloween. It was amazing. They didn't have candy because so many children were on special diets, but they had the coolest toys. They were all dressed up in costumes and many of them had games for the children to play. They had cookies and punch available and it was a really good time for us. Allie got her face painted; one of the most beautiful pink and black butterflies I had ever seen. There were clowns that would make balloon animals and everyone was so kind. On the weekends, there were home improvement stores that would come and bring wood working or tile projects for the children to do. Every weekend, a local business came to the foyer loaded with activities for the children and their siblings to participate in. Allie's absolute favorite, was when they brought the therapeutic dogs to the foyer. She loved to pet and play with them. It was so touching to see people spending their Saturdays and Sundays at the hospital with their dogs, just to make these children smile. The dogs seemed to know what children were having procedures done. They would nuzzle their faces into the children's hands, or lick their faces to try to make them feel better. It was amazing. Allie loved the dogs, she would have stayed all day if she could have, but she could only be away from the video monitoring for 45 minutes at a time. Afterwards, we would go back up to the room and try to do something fun. Often, the people downstairs would let us bring the projects back to our room to complete on our own. That was always fun. They also had volunteers who made blankets for the children. Allie actually still has several of these quilted blankets that reflect the season of the year the child was hospitalized. She has an awesome Halloween blanket that was given to her by a volunteer. There was also a lady, called the pillow lady. This lady, made pillowcases of all different fabric and they were placed on these little pillows that were perfect for little heads. Allie has a couple of these pillows as well. And then, there are the stuffed animals. They must receive donations from everywhere, but it seemed that for every CT or MRI or other procedure that Allie went for, she got to choose a stuffed animal. It was the volunteers and the kind staff at the hospital that made those times more bearable. God puts these people on the planet to reveal his love for us. He gives them the talent and the ability to help children who are stuck in the hospital feel better, and it is through them that He reveals His kindness. It says several times in the Bible that Jesus loves the little children, and I for one firmly believe that.

> *But if anyone has the world's goods and sees his brother in need, yet closes his heart against him, how does God's love abide in him? Little children, let us not love in word or talk but in deed and in truth. 1 John 3:17–18*

CHAPTER 16

·❀·

I received an online message from the physical therapist that was helping Allie when she had her episode at school. She told me that Allie had been blowing on a pinwheel while she was walking through the tunnel. I told the neurologist as soon as he came in what the school therapist had said. He told me that made sense and had he known that missing piece, he might not have asked us to come down. But it was good that we were there because we were ruling out seizure activity; this was a good thing. He instructed us that after he left, we were to have her blow on a pinwheel until she had an episode. He was so attached to her, that he could not stand to see her do it. His nurses called him a chicken as he left and they got Allie a pinwheel. This may have been the most difficult thing I have ever had to do as a parent, so far.

Two nurses were positioned on either side of Allie, who was sitting in a chair. I was sitting on the floor, directly in front of her, so the video camera could capture her reaction. My mother could hardly stand it so she sat way back on to the make shift visitor bed and watched. I did what I will never forget for the rest of my life, I told my daughter to blow on the pinwheel. When she would start to stop, because she was clearly not feeling well, I had to tell her to keep blowing. I had to convince her that it would be okay, she would smile, but I knew she was terrified. She was getting ready to have a mini-stroke and I was making it happen. I kept saying, "Blow, blow baby, keep blowing, don't stop, they need to get brainy to go to sleep. Keep blowing, you're doing good baby, keep blowing," until she finally started going limp. She began falling out of the chair and the nurses caught her just as her head fell forward and her legs buckled underneath her. I burst into tears. She was losing consciousness, and she knew she was going to, but she kept blowing on that stupid pinwheel for me, because I told her to. I had to push my daughter into unconsciousness because they needed to know for sure that she wasn't having seizures. To this day, I will never forget the look on her face when she saw me crying. She started to panic and she began to cry herself, moments into the episode. She saw me crying and was confused and scared. I immediately dried it up and started to tell her that it was okay, she was okay. They wouldn't let me get too close to her, they had to see everything on video and I couldn't block the camera and so I sat within a couple feet of her, unable to comfort her. I sat and watched her slowly come back to us. I told the nurses, "I sure hope you got that because I am never doing that again to her." I had asked her to do something that was totally against her own survival instinct and she did it for me. I had betrayed her; I was supposed to protect her. I will never forget that day, and I will never repeat it.

The neurologist came in the next day to talk to us. He had reviewed the EEG documentation of her episode from the day before and it was certainly not a seizure. He felt confident that she was having Transient Ischemic Attacks (TIA's), not seizures. This was a relief to some degree, although I'm not sure why. In his most professional manner he said, "Her MRI sucks." This was not a relief to any degree. He wanted to move her to the rehab floor so she could get therapy more often and she could participate in all the activities on the floor. She would need to have all of her wires removed and we would be moved as soon as he could get the paperwork put in. I asked him to be candid about her near future. He said he didn't think she would die, but he definitely thought there was a large possibility that she could have a stroke so devastating, that she would have to be taken care of for the rest of her life. He took me to the computer and pulled up her most recent MRI. He showed me the damaged areas of her brain; most of the left side edge was dead as well as about twenty percent of her frontal lobe area. He then began to point out what he called Lacunar infarcts. These were spots deep inside her brain that were damaged from the TIA's. He said, "Honestly she looks a whole lot better than her MRI shows." He wanted to start her on a drug that he had never tried before with children who were having strokes. The drug he wanted to begin her on was called Digoxin. Digoxin is given to heart patients to keep their heart rate up. He was hoping, and this was just a shot in the dark, that when her blood pressure dropped and she had a TIA, that the Digoxin would keep her heart pumping hard enough that the brain would not become deprived of blood and she would avoid a TIA. He also stated that the more he looked at the arteriogram, the more he felt like she had Moyamoya; the same disease that had been ruled out earlier in this nightmare. I had researched it and I could not imagine having to go through life with such a devastating disease. Moyamoya is a progressive disease that is evidenced by the sudden blockage of the large arteries of the brain and replaced by tiny inefficient collateral blood vessels of the brain. The word Moyamoya actually means "puff of smoke", it describes the appearance of these tiny "weblike" blood vessels that shoot blood out from them into the brain that look like a puff of smoke. He wanted to start her on the Digoxin the next day, and trusting him, I said that would be acceptable. Doubts rose and I decided to look into this drug a little closer. I told the doctor who came in to check on her the next day that I didn't want to start her on anything until I had a chance to meet with both her neurologist and the hematologist to find out a little more about this particular drug; a delay that would create another unproductive weekend on the rehab floor of Cook Children's hospital in Fort Worth Texas.

That Monday afternoon, both her neurologist and hematologist met with me in her room while she was at therapy. I asked them point blank, what the risks were of using the Digoxin, what the benefits were, how long she would be on it, if it could permanently affect her heart, and worse, what if it doesn't work. We spoke at length about this particular drug and they assured me that it was safe. They wanted to send her home on Digoxin and Coumadin and wanted me to call them if anything happened or she got worse. I also asked him if there was a possibility that her neurosurgeon could perform another surgery on her. I was desperate to explore every option. He said that he had already discussed that possibility with the neurosurgeon and the neurosurgeon did not want to do any other surgeries on her. She was too small and her blood vessels were much too tiny, less than one millimeter.

"It would be like doing microsurgery," he said.

I asked, "Is there anyone in the country who could do it. Is there anyone anywhere who does these types of surgeries on little ones? Anyone?"

He stopped and thought a minute, and it was the hematologist who said, "You know, I think there are some people in Boston who do it and possibly someone at Stanford who does it." She said, "I believe the guy at Stanford has done it on a baby as young as nine months old."

I was cautiously optimistic and I asked, "Can you please send them our information, just see if she is a candidate for the surgery, just to see?" He of course said that would be no problem, he wanted almost as much as we did to help her. He had become attached to Allie and said that it was very frustrating for him to be unable to help her, to get calls from me and be too far away or ill equipped to help her. I felt helpless as well, but I did have an ally. God was on my side and He had always been there for us. Sometimes it was not on our time table, necessarily, but He definitely knew what He was doing. I also had the idea that He may be deciding that my time with Allie was up. As much as I have always been taught to seek His will, I could not pray it. I couldn't pray it when I was pregnant with the girls, any more than I could do it now. I felt horrible that I didn't have enough trust in God to allow His will. I was too afraid that His will might include taking Allie from me, and as much as I wanted to, I could not ask Him to do it. And so, I prayed for strength and knowledgeable, capable surgeons on the coasts who could help her. I prayed that He would give me more time with her. I thanked Him for the time He had given me, and all of the support He had given us through friends and family. I also prayed that if He was going to take her home that He would give me strength to face it and come to terms with it and feel at peace with the amount of time I was able to spend with her. I was really doing some thinking at the time and I just wanted to spend as much time as possible with her. If she was going to die or be completely incapacitated at some time in the future, I wanted to be with my Allie for as long as I could. As I saw it, I had two choices: quit my job, take her out of school and just spend time with her or just go on with life and let her live it to the fullest. I didn't know what to do. I didn't know what God wanted me to do.

I decided at the time that I could not put her in a plastic bubble and keep her away from everyone and everything. What is life, if she is not able to be a five year old kid? As long as she was in school, I would be there too. I would be teaching, but I would be there with her and I would make every moment count. I would allow her to be a five-year old. She would participate in PE, and play on the playground, eat in the lunch room and carry her own tray, if she could. She would swim at the recreation center and jump on the bed. She would get to live, as long as she was given the chance to live. I also decided that I would try to find those doctors on the coasts who were doing the surgeries. I couldn't waste any time. I was her mother, I was her advocate, I could research Moyamoya, I could find those neurosurgeons that were specializing in helping little children. With God's help, I could do anything. We left Ft. Worth with a new medicine, a new hope and a new mission.

But those who trust in the LORD will find new strength. They will soar high on wings like eagles. They will run and not grow weary. They will walk and not faint. Isaiah 40:31

CHAPTER 17

I began to research Moyamoya on the internet. One particular doctor's name kept popping up, Dr. Gary Steinberg at Stanford University in Palo Alto, California. I looked up a couple of articles on a blog from an individual who had the surgeries, then another blog and a support group for Moyamoya families and their children. I contacted Cook Children's in Fort Worth and asked if they would please refer our case to Dr. Gary Steinberg. The month of November came and went without any word from Texas. At this point, I called them and asked for her MRI's, arteriograms, and CT scans to all be put on disk and mailed to me. This took more time than I would have liked. I had to have them send me a release form so that I could release the information to myself. I waited until I received the form, filled it out and sent it in the very next day. I waited until the disks arrived and I called Dr. Steinberg's office at Stanford University. They were amazing. On the phone, they took all of Allie's information and gave me an address where I could send all of her films for review. They said that Dr. Steinberg would take a look at her films and that someone would call me as soon as they all met and staffed her case. The lady I talked to in the office said that they had a parent advocate whose son had Moyamoya and asked if I would like to talk to her. Of course I agreed and could hardly wait for this mother, who was much like me, to call.

A couple of days went by and the mother, whose son had Moyamoya, called me. We talked about the fears we had for our children, the hospital stays, and then she began to talk about Dr.

Steinberg. She talked about the success rate of his surgeries. She mentioned that her son, in fact had the bypass surgery that Dr. Steinberg does for patients who have Moyamoya all over the world. I was impressed, but skeptical. The phrase too–good–to–be–true kept coming to mind. Was I dreaming up this place that had the potential to help my little girl with the blood flow to her brain? What if he looked at her scans and he said he couldn't help her? What if he said she was too far gone for him to do anything, that I had waited too long to contact him? What if Dr. Steinberg's office calls and said, "I'm sorry Mrs. Marcotte, there isn't anything I can do for your daughter." Even worse, I began to think, what if this place was a scam. A place that would take our money and do her more harm than good. I was terrified of all the unknowns. As so many times before, I turned to God. My prayers were that Dr. Steinberg was real; that he was actually everything the Internet and this mother said he was. I prayed that not only Dr. Steinberg was real but that he would look at Allie's scans and say that she was a perfect candidate for the surgery that would restore blood flow to her brain. I was also praying that she would be one of his success stories.

There were three surgeries that could be performed. The most successful surgery was called the STA-MCA bypass surgery. This surgery was the option that had the most success with patients. The STA-MCA was a direct bypass surgery that allowed the surgeon to isolate an artery and attach it directly to the brain's surface. The other two procedures were both indirect procedures using a muscle graft or a dura graft, and placing them on the surface of the brain allowing the blood vessels from the grafts to grow into the brain and provide blood flow. The direct method works immediately, the indirect method takes six to twelve months. I really wanted Allie to have the direct procedure. This was my prayer for my baby girl who had already been through so much.

I received a late evening call in mid–December from Dr. Steinberg's office. They had met earlier that day and had made a decision about Allie. Waiting for the voice on the other end of the call to give me a verdict, I was almost involuntarily holding my breath. The woman at Dr. Steinberg's office, his nurse, told me that Allie had to have the surgery. She needed bilateral bypass procedures and she needed them as soon as possible. I was a little shocked by this, and asked, "So you think you can actually help her? I mean, she might actually be able to get rid of these TIA's and these strokes?"

"Absolutely," she said. "It is not an option. She has to have the surgery. She does not have enough blood flow to either side of her brain." They asked for our insurance information so that they could get us pre-approved and get everything going so she could be seen right away. The nurse said that a man would be contacting me to give me the schedule so that we could make travel and lodging arrangements. Her sense of urgency scared me but I was ecstatic; it did seem too good to be true. It was brain surgery, very dangerous, invasive, anesthesia for six to eight hours per side; there were a lot of risks to consider. Somehow, though, I had a peace about it. I had a feeling that this is where we were supposed to go. It was a huge victory and an answer to many prayers. But once again, this victory dance would be interrupted.

Two weeks after that exciting call, we received a phone call from the rehab center. The call was left on our answering machine again. It was the collections department that we had dealt with before. The woman on the machine stated that they had made "several attempts to collect payment from both you and your insurance company without any resolution. It is our regret that we will be filing a claim against you in small claims court. You need to call us immediately if you wish to avoid litigation." This was a dark cloud that would not go away. I was frustrated. I had been dealing with these people for more than a year. I had done everything that I knew to do. I had done everything that they had told me to do. I had spent countless hours on the phone with human resources and the insurance company and everyone I talked to described the situation as resolved. Human resources and our insurance company listed our case as "resolved". Apparently, this was not the case for the rehab facility. Because they were unable to collect the $4,000 from our insurance company, they turned to us. Unfortunately, this lead to us reading the local paper and seeing our names listed among at least twenty others being sued in small claims court. I was exhausted and confused, and very angry. Our insurance had paid for everything that Allie had ever needed including brain surgery. She had already been approved at this point for the brain surgery in California. I couldn't understand why they were not paying rehab. The simplest explanation was that they had not been billed correctly. It made perfect sense why they wouldn't pay twice on the same codes. It didn't make sense why the rehab center would bill twice on the same code. The more I thought about it, the more upset I became. They were taking advantage of families who had children with special needs. I refused to let this go. I contacted my local Senator and also wrote a letter to the Insurance Commissioner reporting the rehab facility for fraudulent billing practices. I was getting ready to take my daughter to California for what could possibly amount to a life-saving brain surgery and we were getting sued. Words cannot express how I was feeling. I was going to God in prayer frequently just to keep my thoughts from becoming harmful to myself and my family. I had to be strong for Allie and the others; I couldn't completely lose it now after I'd held it together for so long. I felt like I had been scammed and I had no idea what to do. I went back to placing phone calls to our insurance company and to human resources where my husband worked. Everyone I spoke to was incensed. They could not believe that a place would do this as their common practice, but I believed with all my heart, that was exactly what they did. I did not want anyone else to ever have to go through what I had been through with them. Even my local Senator had said that we were not the first constituents who had told him things like that about them, and that he feared this was a business practice of theirs. I was hopeful that he would follow through and try to do something about it. It is my prayer to this day. I am aware that there are unsavory people in this world, but I am naïve enough to think that I will not cross paths with them. I think somehow that I am immune, when in fact, I am not. God was on our side again, as somehow, the insurance company paid everything they could on the claims, but they could not go back beyond a year of billing. I met with the billing specialist and the co-owner of the center privately. I explained my end of things and how I felt things had just not been billed correctly. They of course both blamed everything on the insurance companies and even stated that they had mailed me bills monthly stating that I still owed them money. I can attest before God that this did not happen and when they both stated that they not only knew the bills were mailed, but saw them go out in the mail, it was apparent that they were in this together and that the meeting was futile. After all of the dust settled, they called me with a new total of $700.00 or a court battle. I drove to the facility and wrote them a check for $700.00. We of course stayed on the court docket until the check cleared but we were finally free. It was like a ten ton weight had been lifted off my shoulder. I could now focus on what was important, my baby girl. Even though I did not get to see justice where this was concerned, I knew that it was not mine to seek justice, it is the Lord's. From experience, I knew that God was much better at dealing out justice than I could ever be. I will never go there and I make sure to never recommend them to anyone I know, but I no longer have terrible thoughts about them. With God's help, I was able to turn my focus completely around to Allie and her upcoming surgeries.

*Yet the **LORD** longs to be gracious to you; he rises to show you compassion. For the **LORD** is a God of justice. Blessed are all who wait for him! Isaiah 30:18*

CHAPTER 18

->✸✿✸<-

We received a call from Mr. Bob Pulliam, the scheduling coordinator in Dr. Steinberg's office during Christmas break of 2009. He wanted to schedule Allie's surgeries for February 4, 2010 and February 11, 2010. He would first do surgery on the left side and then proceed with the right side a week after. Bob informed us that we would be there for no less than three weeks. He mentioned that the hospital had a Ronald McDonald house, but stated that it ran at full capacity. Bob told us that he would be giving us more information as soon as he could schedule all of the tests that needed to be performed before they could do the surgery. She needed another arteriogram, a Doppler flow study, an MRI with and without contrast. They also needed to run a nuclear brain study that uses Diamox to increase blood flow to the brain. The test with Diamox showed them the exact blood vessels that were not getting enough blood flow to the brain. Bob stated that they would run all of the tests before and after her surgeries and we would not be released to go home until our office visit with Dr. Steinberg on February 19, 2010.

I had abandoned the care pages for a more direct form of communication with friends and relatives from around the world. I had a Facebook account and it was through that account that I was able to update people who cared about us on Allie's condition. I posted the plan on my Facebook page and was stunned by the number of people who wanted to help us. I received a call from a parent of one of the children in my class. Sara Moss was interested in helping us fund our trip to California. She and another parent of a child I had years earlier in class, Reva Schumacher, wanted to do some type of a fundraiser that would help us pay for the trip to California. My mother-in-law asked her local sorority to hold an auction and potato dinner to help us with expenses. My aunt on my father's side asked if they could do a garage sale to help pay for Allie's expenses. My cousin, who is an artist, sold paintings and donated the proceeds to us, and my other cousin started an account for people to donate to online at Paypal. It was overwhelming, the amount of support we were receiving. Sara and Reva wanted to do something through a local pizza place. They contacted the paper so that they could do a story on Allie's condition and our experiences. They wanted to help us to open up an account at a local bank in which people from the community could donate money. We were overwhelmed with all of the love and kindness there was in our small, Oklahoma community and from friends and family everywhere. People we hadn't seen in years were sending Allie get well cards with money in them. We would receive anywhere from $5 to $100 in the cards and the account at the bank was filling rapidly. The fundraiser at the pizza place in Claremore was a huge success. So huge, in fact, they had to call in local policemen to help with the traffic flow in and out of the drive-through. The managers said it was their biggest fundraiser to date. The ad in the local paper was on the front page with the cutest picture of Allie. The Headlines read, "A Parent's Worst Nightmare". The garage sales, auctions and donations were much needed as we had to pay for our airfare, housing, meals, hospital bills and copayments as well as medications she would need while she was there. Friends and family wanted desperately to bring meals, help with the kids, clean my house, anything they could do to help us. It was a complete outpouring of God's love for us. The night before we left, I even had a close friend of mine drop by to tell us to be safe, all while she was stuffing a handful of money in my purse, when I wasn't looking. The outpouring of love from our friends, family, our church and this small community was unbelievable.

Love each other with genuine affection and take delight in honoring each other. Romans 12:10

After many prayers of praise and gratitude, I scheduled the flights to Stanford. Mr. Pulliam had instructed us that we needed to be at the Ford Surgery Center by 6:45 a.m. on Monday, January 31. We flew in on Sunday, my mother and I arrived at the airport and took the shuttle to our hotel. We were fairly stressed when we got there because it seemed so far away from the hospital. We hadn't rented a car because neither of us had any desire to drive around a city we were unfamiliar with. The next morning, we took a cab to the hospital. At this point, we were determined to find other housing arrangements closer to the hospital, preferably something that had its own shuttle to and from the hospital. Bringing Allie back to our hotel room after her tests by means of public transportation simply wasn't going to be acceptable. Nervously, we walked up to the desk at the Ford Family Surgery Center and began to cry as we expressed our concerns about being so far away and wanted desperately to talk to someone who could help us find lodging closer to the hospital. The sweet receptionist immediately called and spoke to the doctor who, on our behalf, called the Ronald McDonald house and got us right in. Allie's procedure started about four hours late and my little girl was again hungry and miserable. We tried everything we knew to help her get her mind off of food. She was checked in and in her hospital gown, all ready for her arteriogram. The arteriogram was a procedure that she had twice before, both times at Cook Children's hospital. We knew the drill, we knew all of the risks, how she would have to be sedated, and how she would have to be still for six hours following the procedure. We were not looking forward to it, but it was something that simply had to be done. As the fourth hour of the delay came and went, our patience began to wear thin. Eventually, we signed all of the papers and she was wheeled back into the procedure room. Mom and I walked back to the visitor's waiting room where we would wait for news that she was finished. I had brought my laptop to the hospital so I could update everyone on Facebook. There were thousands of prayers being said for Allie and for us as we were going through, what the Claremore newspaper termed, "A Parent's Worst Nightmare." I think the nightmare part of the experience was the not knowing. The not knowing was the part that made us crazy. Going day to day, wondering if this would be our last day to be with her. That was the nightmare we were living. I was in constant prayer during these times, often finding a quiet corner to close my eyes and speak to my Lord.

Two hours later, we were escorted out of the waiting room and into the recovery room where Allie was stirring, starting to wake up. We knew she would be hungry and thirsty and we were prepared to advocate for her to be able to eat as soon as possible. A peculiar thing about Allie was that she always woke from these types of procedures asking for spaghetti to eat. It always made us smile, because it seemed to be her way of saying, "I'm okay—I'm fine, I am hungry for spaghetti." Convincing the staff of the Ford Surgery Center that she was ready for spaghetti was an entirely different matter. They always had an order in which they introduced foods to the patient; they began with ice chips, then popsicles, and other clear liquids. Next they would transition her to solids such as crackers or dry cookies, and if she could hold all of that down, they allowed her to have real food. Allie had no time for such a ridiculous order of things. She would eat the ice chips and ask for spaghetti. She would eat the crackers and again ask for spaghetti. We were blessed that she did not get nauseous from the anesthesia, but the process was always the same. Eventually, we would move on to spaghetti but not without bending the rules a bit. The nurses in recovery would bring us Spaghetti-O's from their stash of things they kept in their private pantry. Allie was thrilled. After she was able to hold down the Spaghetti-O's we were transitioned to the short-term stay unit of the hospital. This is where we had to hold her still for six hours so that she would not bleed out of the major artery in her leg. We were thankful that the hospital had televisions and movies that Allie could choose from all hours of the day and night. It was during this time, that we were informed that the doctor had secured us a room at the Ronald McDonald house.

There were many rules for staying at the Ronald McDonald house, our least favorite of which was no food or drink in the rooms. This would definitely put a kink in our plans. Televisions were also not allowed in the rooms and there was only one queen size bed for the three of us for the next three weeks. Our enthusiasm was undeterred and I was happy to get into a place that was near enough to the hospital that I could literally walk there and back. It may have been a half a mile either way but I loved walking, and the weather in Palo Alto was excellent. God had answered our prayers again and it seemed like things were definitely turning in our favor. And yet again, small victories were short lived and quickly replaced with complications.

As if things were not stressful enough, things were about to get more complicated; not with Allie, not with doctors or medicine and not with insurance companies. Nothing can match the complications of family.

CHAPTER 19

My parents both love Allie and all of my children dearly and would do anything in the world for them. However, their divorce and subsequent bitterness left them unable to be in the same room with each other. This created many awkward moments. My dad was extremely worried about Allie and two weeks prior to our leaving home for California, he contacted me. My dad wanted to know if he could help us out while we were there. He had a motor home that he was willing to drive from his home in Austin, Texas, and was happy to drive us to and from the hospital in his car. He was happy to let us stay in the motor home for as long as we needed to. He wanted to be there for Allie, he was very worried about her and wasn't completely sure that she would make it through this. I spoke to my mom about it before we left Oklahoma. I knew it was imperative that my mom accompany me to California. Allie would not tolerate anyone taking care of her in the hospital except me or my mom. Allie wanted me to never leave her side, but that wasn't possible if I ever wanted to eat, take a shower, or go to the bathroom. I need my mom so that she could sit with Allie during the times that I needed a break. I also was hoping that should something have happened to Allie and she take a turn for the worse that my mother would have been there for me. I spoke to my mom about her ex-husband's offer to help us out while we were there. She sternly said, "If he drives out there then I am not going." It was again, a situation that to me was intolerable; how could one be there for Allie and me to the exclusion of the other? I decided I needed mother there, more than I needed to continue the negotiations at hand. I called my dad and told him that despite the generous nature of his offer, I would have to decline it so that Allie would have my mother to sit with if I needed to be somewhere else. A week later my father informed me that despite my need to decline, he was no longer under the direct orders of my mother and if he wanted to drive to California, he was over twenty-one years of age and free to do so at his discretion. My daughter was about to have brain surgery and I had this to deal with as well. My father was going to be in California at the same time and if my mother knew this, she would refuse to go with us. I felt like there could be no winner in such a situation, least of all Allie. My dad was gracious enough to tell me that he would not go to the hospital without my permission and that he would stay out of our way. His concern was primarily Allie and her treatment and recovery. He was worried however, that it might not go as planned and that he would need to be there for me. I prayed that God would show me the answer to this dilemma. I needed His guidance more than ever. I felt very guilty about not telling my mother the truth but Allie and I needed her in California. Not that my dad isn't a good person, but Allie wouldn't be as comfortable staying with him and allowing me to do anything or go anywhere without her. I knew there would be repercussions; I knew my mom would find out, I knew there would be a confrontation. I was just praying that it would not hinder my ability to support Allie and that it would not interfere with her ability to heal and get back home. I wanted to focus just on Allie and not on my parents. And I expected the same from them. My cup was almost completely full and I wasn't sure I could do much more in the way of being a gracious person.

We had to get to the Ronald McDonald House before 5:00 p.m. to fill out the paperwork and get the key to our room. I had to get to our hotel room and retrieve our belongings and get us moved into the Ronald McDonald House, while mom sat with Allie. Mom didn't feel capable of doing all of that on her own, and so she volunteered to stay with Allie while I took care of everything. I was on a mission to retrieve our luggage and get us moved in to the Ronald McDonald house as soon as possible. I halfway listened to the instructions the nurse gave me on the public transit system (bus routes) and decided, partially because I was starving and partially because I was sick of it all, that I would call my dad and have him pick me up around the corner from the hospital. Allie hadn't had her surgery yet and I really didn't want it all to blow up in my face before we got the worst of this behind us. I called my dad and he immediately picked me up about a quarter mile from the hospital entrance. I entered the car and thanked him for picking me up. I also thanked him for being so discreet and allowing me to be selfish and get as much support as I could during this time. He took me straight to the hotel and helped me gather the luggage and check-out. He drove me to the Ronald McDonald House where we filled out the paperwork, got the tour and settled in with all of our things. I had not eaten anything since breakfast and it was nearing dinner time. I asked if we could get something to eat, he took me to dinner and I told him how Allie was doing. We talked about the week ahead of us and I promised him I would call him and keep him up to date. After dinner, he drove me back to the hospital. I felt so much better knowing we were set up at the Ronald McDonald House and knowing that we would get to stay there that night. When I got to the room, Allie was watching a movie while my mom sat in the chair beside her. The nurse came in and said that she only had a few more hours to go before she would be released and as long as she didn't run a fever we would be able to leave. Of course, I had learned by now not to count my chickens until they are hatched; an appropriate Oklahoma phrase. Allie began running a slight fever just before we were to be released and unfortunately the doctor on call decided we would be spending the night there. I was exhausted and a little defeated. I had mom catch the last shuttle from the hospital to the Ronald McDonald House so one of us could be well rested tomorrow. I told her to go ahead and get things ready for us to come by in the morning. Allie was scheduled for another procedure the next day, one that required she have nothing to eat or drink after midnight. My night would again be spent sleeping in a chair next to my baby girl, waiting for her fever to go away so that we could leave the hospital. We had so been looking forward to spending the night in the Ronald McDonald House; anything was better than spending another night in another hospital.

The next morning, mom came up to visit us. She had eaten breakfast but I had given her the heads up about Allie not being able to eat, and so she had wisely decided not to bring me anything to eat or drink. That was our policy; if Allie couldn't eat, then we didn't eat.

We thought it was rude to eat or drink in front of her. She was only five and not able to understand why she couldn't have anything to eat or drink. She awoke fussy and hungry but we made it out of there in time for our next appointment.

Once again we all gathered at the check-in area of the Ford Family Surgery center. For this procedure, Allie would need anesthesia for the nuclear brain study with Diamox. Again, a delay of nearly three hours past her appointment time caused unneeded stress. We were all wearing thin of our patience and we were very hungry. Once they took Allie, mom and I were able to get something to eat at the hospital cafeteria. The procedure was to take less than two hours so we hurried back and waited for news that she was again in recovery. They came out and said she was starting to wake up and that everything had gone well. We met her in recovery where we, once again, started the introduction of post procedure foods. Again, she asked for spaghetti, but we had cleaned them out the day before of Spaghetti-O's. We just wanted to get out of there in time to catch the last shuttle to the Ronald McDonald House. We passed all the ice chips, clear fluids and cracker tests and were released to go. We stopped at the cafeteria and got her some dinner before catching the shuttle to the Ronald McDonald House. She was so happy to be out of the hospital, she ran all over the room, rolling around on the bed, anxious to watch television. We made our first trip to the common area where there was a television. Mom and Allie commenced to watching something semi-interesting as I plugged in my laptop to posts the day's events on my Facebook page. It had been an exhausting last couple of days and tomorrow would be no exception.

Allie was scheduled for her nuclear imaging study without Diamox, and her MRI with and without contrast. Again, she would be unable to have anything to eat or drink after midnight. Our prayer that evening was that everything would run on time this time. It was bad enough that she was going without food for such long periods while being on-time for her procedures, but three and four hours past her scheduled procedure time was unacceptable. It was making an intolerable situation even more intolerable. All the while, my dad was in the city reading my Facebook pages and trying to stay out my mother's way. It was a little more than my fragile emotional state could handle. I stayed in prayer most of the time and God furnished me with the needed strength. Not having a television in the room helped dramatically. I had a book I was reading about forgiveness and faith and that helped me to stay upbeat and positive.

My mom didn't feel comfortable sleeping in the queen size bed with Allie and me so we went down stairs in search of an air mattress that she would sleep on. We were in luck, they had one left and we were welcomed to use it. We took it upstairs, inflated it and got prepared to get on the bus the next morning to Allie's next appointment. The next day would be Allie's last set of tests before her surgery was scheduled that Thursday the fourth of February. Again, she could have nothing to eat or drink after midnight. We were growing tired of Allie being put through so much. My mother was struggling with her asthma and she was developing a cough. It was right in the middle of flu season and the hospital was very picky about who they let in. Coughing or any other noticeable symptom would be enough to deny access into the hospital to visit for any reason. I was praying that mom's cold or whatever it was she had would go away, I needed her with me for support, just in case anything happened during Allie's surgeries.

We made it to check in at the Ford Surgery Center for the third and final tests before her surgery. Again, we were hopeful that her procedures would be on time, and again, they ran two hours late. These two tests would take approximately two hours and we knew that she would likely be asking for spaghetti when she got up. I really wanted her to have something good to eat before her surgery the next day. I told my mom that I was sure if I called the Ronald McDonald House and gave them my dad's credit card number that maybe a volunteer would run to Olive Garden, Allie's favorite, and bring us some dinner. Mom thought that was a great idea so I left the surgery waiting room and made the call . . . to my dad. I justified my actions because it was for Allie, and because it seemed silly that he wasn't able to be in the same city with us. Of course, my dad was more than happy to do it. Again, Allie's tests went well and she passed the ice chip, Popsicle, cracker test and we were off to the shuttle. When we got back that evening to the Ronald McDonald House, there was dinner from the Olive Garden waiting at the front desk. Allie was thrilled. She enjoyed every bite of her spaghetti and we retired to our room, exhausted and ready for the next day to be over. My mother's cough seemed to be getting worse and I worried constantly that she would not be allowed into the hospital or, even worse, that we would be kicked out of the Ronald McDonald House because she was "sick". Throughout the night, mom's air mattress would lose air and we would hear her turn the pump on to pump it back up. This happened every three to four hours throughout the evening, every evening for three weeks. The air mattress fiasco proved to be one of those frustrating moments that would be remembered and laughed about years later.

The next morning was Allie's surgery. It would be an early surgery that was expected to take between six and eight hours, just for one side of her brain. They told us that they wouldn't know exactly what he could do for her until he opened her up and looked in there. Allie and I woke up early and got ready to go. I could tell that mom wasn't feeling well and so I told her to stay, get some rest and come later that morning to the hospital. The shuttle ran every thirty minutes and she could easily catch another one. The last thing we needed was for her to get sick, especially with her asthma. It wouldn't be the first time she would have to be admitted to the hospital for her asthma and I wasn't completely sure I could handle both of them being hospitalized and me there by myself. I told mom that I would see if the Ronald McDonald House had a volunteer who could bring her some cough medicine and some things that might help her feel better. Again, I called my dad from the hospital and he brought everything on my list right away to the front desk. I felt bad about being so dishonest with my mom, but I also was in survival mode. I was doing what I had to do for myself and for Allie. I was certain, if my mom knew my dad was there, she would get even sicker, or quit talking to me, or worse they would break out into a fight in the middle of the hospital. There was no way I could handle any of those things right now and so I continued to be dishonest with my mother about my dad being in Palo Alto. I prayed to God for forgiveness and hoped that He understood how my intentions were directed. I was not proud of myself but I was not about to put Allie, or my mother, through any kind of distress that could be avoided.

> **But if anyone does not provide for his relatives, and especially for members of his household, he has denied the faith and is worse than an unbeliever. 1 Timothy 5:8**

CHAPTER 20

—✤—

Allie and I checked in again at the Ford Family Surgery Center. This was the big day; the day I had been praying about for months. They were doing surgery on the left side first, the side that had the most damage and the least amount of blood flow. I was praying for some miracle that he would find an artery big enough to be able to do the direct bypass. I knew this was her best option. I also knew that once an indirect procedure was performed on a child of her size, a direct bypass was no longer possible. I knew that this was our one and only chance. I had been keeping everyone updated through my Facebook page and I knew that there were hundreds of people praying for her throughout her surgery. From time to time, I would get a text asking for an update and I would post it again on Facebook. Mom arrived at the hospital after they had already taken her back for her procedure and we waited together. We were both exhausted although mom seemed to be feeling better. We had been getting up early every morning and getting to bed late in the evening since we had been here and I was sure that neither one of us had adjusted to the time difference. Every once in a while, Allie's surgical nurse would come out and tell us how she was doing. The reports were always positive, but she did tell us that it did not look like he would be able to do the direct by-pass. Her arteries were just too tiny. She told us that he was still looking for a good artery and that he would not give up easily. I could feel the prayers of everyone who cared about us. I knew beyond a shadow of a doubt, that Allie would be okay. I again had a profound sense of peace for someone who was almost completely without family and friend's physical presence, and miles away from home in a strange hospital. Six hours later, it was over. Dr. Steinberg came in to tell us what he did and how she was doing. He said that despite his best efforts, he was unable to find an artery large enough to do a direct bypass procedure on her. He did however, take a large portion of the dura, a dense tissue covering the brain, and "flip" it, placing it over her brain as a way of drawing blood to her brain. This was an indirect procedure and would take at least six months before we saw any changes in her TIA activity. I was disappointed but was extremely glad it was over. I felt at that point, that I had done everything that I could. She was being moved to PICU and they would call when she was settled. It was then that we met her PICU nurse "Edith".

Edith was a nurse who busied herself constantly and was extremely concerned about the rules and procedures of the hospital. We had just arrived in the PICU and she began immediately scolding us, "You do not touch the baby. You do not kiss the baby on the mouth. No cell phones, food or drink in the ward. You wash your hands before and after you touch anything in the room. Do not put anything on the floor, especially your purses. You are not allowed to be in the ward during shift change or report. You must leave the ward to sleep in the designated sleep spaces. You are not my concern, your daughter is my responsibility and I will make sure that she is taken care of." I looked at mother and she had started to cry, I was shaking and I also started to cry. I had no idea what I had done to provoke this nurse to begin her tirade, but I was terrified. I knew Allie's reaction when I left her, I also knew that I had no intention of leaving her and I immediately felt helpless. These people, this hospital that I had picked out for my daughter on-line had a terrible policy with regard to families. I couldn't believe it. The social worker came in and introduced herself to us and she immediately saw us crying. We told her what the nurse had said and she immediately began to try to comfort us. She gave me the number of my sleep space on the floor above the PICU. The space had four beds, each were reserved for a family member who was there with someone in the PICU. There was a kitchen and a shared bathroom that had a shower in it. It sounded wonderful but I knew for sure that I was not staying in my sleep space. I was staying with my daughter that night and if they had to throw me out, they would just have to do that. I was not moving.

Allie was asking for crackers and I remember that Edith had shown me the snack area of the ward and told me to help myself for Allie. I began to leave the private room we were in when suddenly, I saw Edith angrily heading in my direction. She yelled, "No, no momma, you get back in there, you cannot come out of the room while we are giving report." I quickly turned around and went into the room. I was again scared to death to do anything. I got the attention of a different nurse who looked friendly and told her what happened. She immediately went to the snack station and retrieved some crackers for Allie. It was as if this nurse knew that Edith was a problem. Edith lacked basic social skills. It would seem that surely she was good at her job, however, she had established absolutely no rapport with me or my mother; in fact we were scared to death of her. There are certain things that I tried very hard not to do and one very important thing was that I never wanted to make my daughter's caregivers angry. I knew that upsetting the people who were taking care of my child would not be in our best interest. I prayed and continued to be patient with Edith, and I tried my very best to just stay out of her way. My mother couldn't take it and she left. Allie was awake and was asking to speak to her daddy on the phone. I poked my head out of the room and asked Edith, if Allie could call her daddy in Oklahoma. She said, "I said you can't use the cell phone, she can call anyone she wants."

I had been given the number for the surgical nurse who had become attached to Allie before surgery. I called her immediately and asked for her advice. She contacted Dr. Steinberg and told him that we needed out of the PICU as soon as possible. The stay is typically two days in PICU and two days on the floor. There was no way we would be able to stay more than one terrifying night in the PICU. I had never been told that I could not stay with my daughter after any procedure. I moved my chair to the corner of the room, covered myself in a blanket and tried to be as quiet as possible. I spent the entire night scared to death, that they would ask me to leave my baby there alone and that I would have no other choice, but to leave. That night, after Edith's shift ended, I immediately felt better. I called my dad and asked him if he wanted to come by and see Allie. I told him that mother had already gone back to the Ronald McDonald House and that it would be safe for him to come and visit her. I figured that Allie might possibly divulge his presence to mother, but it was worth taking the chance. I was a nervous wreck between Edith the "psycho nurse", my mother's hatred of my father, and Allie's brain surgery.

My dad came up and stayed only a few minutes, enough time to see if I was okay and to give Allie a kiss on the forehead. I hid myself in the chair overnight, trying not to fall asleep. If I was sleeping, I had to go to the sleep space; I could stay as long as I was awake. I posted on Facebook about our "psychotic nurse" and everything I was feeling. I didn't go into detail on the Internet, but I knew I would be corresponding with the hospital administration when this was all over. I didn't want even one other family being scared out of their wits by this woman. It was easy to stay awake, the PICU was loud and the lights were on the entire night. I wondered if all the bright lights and loud voices were what a child that had just come from brain surgery needed to heal right now. I started to mentally document all of my concerns so that I could accurately express them to the hospital administrators, and Dr. Steinberg's office. I was certain, that he had no idea what went on here in the PICU.

We had made it through the night, and a new nurse came on at 7:00 a.m. I was relieved that it was not Edith. I expressed my concerns about Edith and relayed to our new nurse everything that had happened the day before. She remained professional, but I could tell she had heard this before. She immediately went to the charge nurse and had them put in Allie's chart that Edith could not be our nurse again. I was instantly relieved and our new nurse was very kind. She did have to tell us that Allie was scheduled for an MRI today and so would be unable to eat breakfast until after her MRI. I couldn't believe that she would not be able to eat again. I was feeling very frustrated, I was exhausted both mentally and physically and I wasn't sure how much more of this I could take. I called mom and told her to take her time coming up. I told her that Allie wasn't allowed to eat until after her MRI this morning, so that she wouldn't bring us any breakfast. I was hungry, but I was more tired than anything. One of the most difficult parts of being in a hospital is trying to convince your five year old that she would have to wait for a procedure to be finished before she could eat. She was having pain in her head and wanted her IV's out and I could tell that her resolve was wearing thin.

I called on my prayer warriors again for help. I felt like a "prayer-hog", as if there were only a finite number of prayers God could hear, and I was being selfish asking for more.

They came up around 1:00 p.m. and took her for her MRI. I was starving. Mom and I went to the cafeteria to eat, get some caffeine and a brief sanity check. We had to get out of the PICU before nightfall. The nurses had assured us that Dr. Steinberg wanted her moved to the floor and they were doing everything they could to get us there. There weren't any available rooms on the floor and we were stuck in the PICU until they could get us a room. Allie had finished her MRI and was back in the PICU alert and of course, hungry. The menu that day was pizza; Allie was so happy. Whenever Allie was happy, I was elated. Just to see her happily eat her pizza and watch a movie gave me strength to keep going. I knew that as long as she was being strong, I could be strong for her. God provided that.

The nurses immediately began moving us out of our private room and into what I call "general population". General population was noisy and full of lights and the sounds of about six other patients echoed through the shared room. We were separated by curtains but shared one nurse with three other patients. There was barely enough room for one guest in general population, but two was really pushing it. I found myself sitting at the bottom of Allie's bed, which Allie really preferred anyway. I just knew we had to get moved to a room on the floor before midnight. I wasn't completely sure they would let me stay with Allie in such a crowded area.

As night approached, I began to feel scared again. I did not want to leave her there alone, I did not want to go to my sleep space on the next floor and I wanted to get moved out of the PICU. Allie began fussing loudly about her IV hurting her. A kind nurse checked her intake and output of fluids and decided she no longer needed her IV; a quick answer to a continued prayer. It was painful to watch her suffer, to watch her fuss and cry because she was tired or hungry. Anything that anyone did to help her be more comfortable was greatly appreciated.

At approximately 1:30 a.m., we were moved to a room on the floor. Although semi-private separated by a curtain, there was a sleep space in the room for me. There was a sweet little baby in the room beside us. It was a relief to be there. Instead of the beeps of machines, and the loud voices we got to hear the soft voice of a mother singing lullabies to the baby next to us. This baby's name was also Allison and she was discharged that next morning to go home. I was jealous and happy for her at the same time. I wanted this whole experience to be over.

Allie reached her breaking point just after breakfast that morning. She was screaming and crying and thrashing in the bed. It was a good thing that the monitors were not on her because her blood pressure would have been through the roof. We contacted Dr. Steinberg's fellow and begged to get released. The on-call neurologist came by to look at Allie before discharging us. He immediately noticed that her IV was gone and he began to interrogate me. He wanted to know who had removed her IV; he wanted a name to report her. I told him that the kind nurse who removed her IV had done us a favor and that I would not give him any information about the person who made such a heroic decision for us. He wanted her IV put back in as it would be another 45 minutes before we would be discharged and it was strict procedure that her IV stayed in her arm until the exact time of discharge. He left, and I immediately told the nurse that there was no way he or anyone else was going to start an IV on her that would be in for 45 minutes. I knew we had to get out of there. I also knew that we would have to be back in a week for the exact same thing and I was again scared to death. Common sense and calmer heads prevailed and we were able to avoid another IV.

We were released with our Tylenol and our Neosporin for the suture line on her head. She was developing a little cough from the past four days of anesthesia, but nothing that would keep us in the hospital. We were ready to go to the Ronald McDonald House. We loaded up and caught the shuttle back to our home away from home. Allie was asking for chips and salsa so I contacted my dad outside while mom and Allie watched a movie on the computer. He brought it within the hour and Allie had her chips and salsa. While we were in the hospital, my dad had also stocked our refrigerator and pantry with cereal, chocolate milk, Hershey bars and Kit Kat bars. For me, he stocked the fridge with Dr. Pepper and left a bag full of shampoo and other personal items that would help us feel more at home during our stay. Dad's presence in California was a true blessing.

There were always activities going on at the Ronald McDonald House. Each evening they had various businesses around town that brought in dinner. On Thursdays, the shuttle would take families to Target or Wal-Mart for essentials. Allie's surgeries were always on Thursdays so we only seemed to be able to take that trip once. We were there during Valentine's Day and a local group brought all kinds of craft foam hearts and beads to make valentines for family and friends. We also had a group bring scrapbooking supplies one particular evening. I was especially excited about this. I loved to scrapbook and anything I could do to take my mind off the week's events was a relief.

We were even treated each morning to cupcakes from a local cupcake store that was quite popular. Across the street from the Ronald McDonald House was an amazingly beautiful upscale mall. The least expensive store, apart from McDonalds was Gap and we would window shop from time to time. The house had an umbrella stroller that I could borrow so Allie and I could enjoy the fresh air. The mall had a beautiful water fountain and on Sundays people brought their dogs to the mall to shop with them. Allie especially loved seeing all the dogs. She had missed her pets at home very much. Three dogs, two cats, one guinea pig and one fish were at home away from us, so we both enjoyed seeing the dogs at the mall. Occasionally, someone would allow Allie to pet their animal and it was difficult to drag her away. The Ronald McDonald House had people come on varying days with animals. One particular volunteer had brought in a Labrador retriever. We both just hugged and petted that dog like she was our own. I began to cry as thoughts of home became very clear. We weren't even close to going home; she still had another surgery to go, and then all of the tests all over again. At one point, a local group brought bunnies, a pony and a couple of turtles to the house in the back yard and Allie was again completely happy. She got to hold the bunnies and pet them, it was so therapeutic. The House also had BINGO night complete with donated kid prizes and toys. Allie won a DS game that had horses on it. She was having fun outside of the hospital and I was extremely grateful for that. Not only were we being spoiled at the Ronald McDonald House, but we were getting boxes of goodies every other day. Allie's kindergarten class mailed her cards and a giant banner that said "Get Well Allie". We hung it over our bed, she loved it. Other classes had gathered soaps and lotions, gum and snack items. We loved the snack items the most. It was the one thing we could eat in the room while we relaxed and watched videos on the computer. Every once in a while, mom would walk over to the mall with us and buy Allie a shirt from Gap. Allie loved it when her "memaw" would go, because she knew memaw would get her something cool from the mall. I enjoyed the walking more than anything. I was a kindergarten teacher who typically didn't sit down for hours, and I was stuck in a room where there wasn't a whole lot to do. The Ronald McDonald House was an answer to prayer. God made sure that we were as comfortable as possible while we were dealing with all of this uncertainty.

We did have to deal with some fire alarms that always seemed to occur in the middle of the night. By the third fire alarm, my mother announced that she was not moving and that the fire would just have to consume her. It was a pain, grabbing your sleeping baby and running down two flights of stairs into the cold air of the night without any jackets. It was always the same person to blame, someone in one of the quarantined apartments who had left their stove on causing the alarm to trigger. By the third alarm from the same person, we were left wondering what exactly you would have to do to get evicted. However, we were not willing to take that chance. We were happy there. With my dad on speed dial, bringing us anything we needed, we were actually quite spoiled. With God on our side, we had more than we could ever ask.

> *The Lord is my Shepherd; I shall not want.*
> *He maketh me to lie down in green pastures:*
> *He leadeth me beside the still waters. He restoreth my soul:*
> *He leadeth me in the paths of righteousness for His name's sake.*
> *Psalm 23: 1–3*

CHAPTER 21

The time had come for us to go back to the hospital for Allie's second surgery. I was very nervous this time. I was hopeful that it would go better than the first surgery and that Dr. Steinberg would be able to do a direct bypass on her right side. I hated to put her through everything again and I wondered what she would do when she figured out we were going back. Another blessing was ours as she willingly got into the shuttle to go back to the hospital to get the other half of "brainy" fixed. We checked in at the Ford Family Surgery Center and waited a relatively short time before she was taken back to surgery. Mom and I again went to the cafeteria for breakfast, as had become our tradition. We knew that this surgery would again be roughly six hours and we were in no hurry to get back to the crowded waiting room. I wasn't at all excited about the idea of going back to the PICU and possibly another episode with my least favorite nurse of all time—Edith.

Dr. Steinberg came out almost six hours after the procedure had started and stated that she had done well. He said that as before, he was unable to do a direct bypass as she had no arteries that were bigger than one millimeter in diameter. This was a bit deflating. He had used a part of her temporal muscle this time to revascularize the right side of her brain and was hopeful that this would make a difference for her in the upcoming months. While we had his attention, I pleaded with him to let us go to a room on the floor. I told him that I hated the PICU, it was so restrictive and loud. He politely refused, insisting that she was required to have someone watching her very closely for the first 24 hours. He assured me however, that he would get us out of there as soon as he could, as long as she was doing well. I was so nervous and apprehensive. We met Allie in the PICU as soon as she was there and settled. I looked around and saw no sign of Edith. I liked our nurse immediately and made sure to let her know that we could not have Edith under any circumstances. She assured us that we were not the only ones who had voiced concerns about Edith. Her words made us feel better but there was still an uneasy concern about why Edith was still a nurse who interfaced with patients and families at such a stressful time. I made a vow that day to not let this go. I was determined to write a letter with several copies going to key people there at the hospital. I wanted my feelings and my perspective known. I had been to four different hospitals in three states over a two year period; I felt my opinions should be valid.

Allie was much more swollen this time around her eyes and her head. She had somewhat of a black eye on that right side. She also seemed to be in a lot more pain this time. They gave her morphine for the first few hours and switched her to hydrocodone after that. She wasn't allowed to eat anything heavy after the surgery, but because she felt so bad, she wasn't asking for food. We put a movie on for her, but she slept a lot from the painkillers. The nurse assured me that they would not throw me out of the PICU that night. When the social worker came to give me my bed number for the sleep space, I declined it and told her to give it to someone else. The nurse was kind and understood how I was feeling. She said she would feel the same way if it was her child and that she actually felt better, if a parent was in the room with the child. Allie slept so much, that she missed dinner and slept all the way through the night. After my mom left to catch the last shuttle to the Ronald McDonald House, I called my dad to have him come up to see her. When he arrived, he told me that he thought he had seen my mom just outside the front doors to the hospital. I was relieved when he said that she had not seen him. I had at least another night in this hospital and I still needed my mother's support. I was exhausted and hungry and would be without any future breaks, unless mom could sit with Allie. I knew it was only a matter of time before mom figured out that my dad was here and I knew I had to figure something out. Allie wanted very badly to go to a beach and we had no way of taking her there. I knew my dad would be more than happy to take her to the beach, but I also knew that this would require my secret to be revealed. I felt guilty for lying and continuing to deceive my mom. I felt like I was being selfish by having them both there, but I also knew that my actions were completely based on what was best for Allie. She had been able to eat chips and salsa and spaghetti because my dad was here. I knew that the only way Allie was going to see a beach was with my dad driving us there, all of us.

Dad stayed for only a few minutes and he brought me a strawberry cream drink from Starbucks. I was starving and hadn't eaten since breakfast and I was extremely grateful for the drink. He gave Allie a kiss on the forehead, hugged me goodbye and left for the evening. I could tell how relieved he was that she was doing well and that nothing had gone wrong during the surgeries. I was also very relieved that the most difficult times were now behind us. I was looking forward to the future; a future that would hopefully be free of these awful mini-strokes, and a future that would be completely void of the feeling that she could die at any moment from a massive stroke. I was ready to put all of this behind us and move forward as a family. I gathered a blanket around me and sat on the chair in the corner again, trying not to be noticed, just in case Edith was running around somewhere on the PICU.

The next morning, Allie was not allowed to eat until after her MRI, again. She was very hungry since she hadn't eaten anything at all the day before and I started to get stressed again. I knew that if her MRI wasn't timely today, we would see another fit of gargantuan proportion. Again, I found myself in prayer that God would help the MRI to be on time so that she could eat very soon. I thanked Him for such smooth and gifted surgical hands and the kind nurses he had given us for Allie's care. And I thanked Him that we had been surrounded by friends and family during this time through Facebook. I felt blessed that I could go to the computer and post my fears, my joys, and Allie's progress and see responses that made me feel loved and supported. It was like having everyone there with me. It was definitely a blessing. We were blessed beyond measured the entire time we were there. Sometimes, we had to look hard to see the blessings, but they were there, we just had to look.

Allie's MRI got pushed back into the afternoon and the nurse came in with apple juice and popsicles for her. I knew it wouldn't be too much longer before Allie's patience was tested. I was hopeful that she would get into the MRI before too long and we could move on and get ourselves moved to a floor room. Her hair was a disaster. There was no getting a comb through it and her head hurt badly enough from the surgery that she would be in terrible pain if I tried to comb it. She couldn't wash it for another three days. It would just have to wait. Thankfully they came to take her around 2:30 in the afternoon. While she was in the MRI, they were moving us to general population, again. General population was rough; luckily it wasn't nearly as crowded as the week before. We gathered our things while she was in the MRI and moved ourselves to our new space. I left mom there and went to get myself some breakfast. I made my way to the cafeteria and grabbed a bite to eat. I also decided to make a call to Dr. Steinberg's assistant, Nadia, from Switzerland. She was an amazing woman who had bonded with Allie during the last couple of weeks. She had actually written two children's books on Moyamoya and had given us a signed copy of each of them. I called her and asked her if we could please be moved to the floor as soon as possible. After making some calls, she contacted me to tell me that there were just no rooms on the floor. I asked her if we could possibly be released today to go back to the Ronald McDonald House. It had only been 24 hours since surgery and I knew it was a long shot. She called Dr. Steinberg who told her "no way". She asked him if it was possible for us to be released from the PICU the next day, Dr. Steinberg told her he would consider it.

Allie came back from her MRI to general population where we had been moved. She was starving and she wasn't taking "no" for an answer. She devoured some crackers from the pantry and drank some apple juice. We knew she wouldn't last long with those and so we ordered a tray from the hospital cafeteria. She was treated to a cheeseburger and fries. She ate like a champion. We were so thankful that she never got sick after the procedures. She had received anesthesia so many times and eaten heartily after every procedure but never once got sick. Vomiting after brain surgery was frowned upon. I know that was why they were so strict about it. Vomiting strains the body enough to split a stitch or detach a new tissue or even cause bleeding in the brain after surgery. The doctors and nurses knew that it was worse for her to get sick right after surgery. I still hated every time she had to go without food for long periods. After everything I had seen her go through, depriving her of food and drink just seemed cruel.

Mom left for the evening to go back to the Ronald McDonald House and I called my dad to see if he wanted to come up for a visit. Dad didn't stay long, but I did bring up the possibility of him taking us to the beach. Of course he was delighted to do it but knew that mom would be unhappy with him being there. We had however, made it through the worst part of the trip and if mom got too angry and decided to just sit in the room at the Ronald McDonald House; I might be able to handle it. However a full scale argument or confrontation with someone who was angry wasn't exactly something I needed. I needed a plan. I needed a plan that would get Allie to a beach and keep everybody happy. I had a lot of experience being the peacekeeper in the family. My mom and my sister were constantly getting into fights that I had to referee. I didn't like family conflict and I just preferred to keep the peace. I knew however, that it wasn't always possible. I wanted to do everything I could to keep everybody happy and do what was best for Allie. My dad left for the evening and I grabbed a blanket and sat in the chair beside her bed as quietly as possible. There was still a chance that the nurse coming on at 11:00 p.m. would order me out and I couldn't take that chance.

The next morning, Nadia came in to tell us that we would be discharged from the PICU. Allie looked great and she was eating and drinking and there was really no reason to stay. The hospital staff all seemed to agree that children did better on the floor of the hospital but with no rooms available, the next best thing would be to discharge us. We were ecstatic. I called mom and let her know that we would be coming home soon. I was experienced enough to know that anytime you were being discharged; it meant at least another three hours or more in the hospital. Still, we were happy that there was a light at the end of our tunnel and that by far, the worst of this trip was behind us. The nurses knew that we had another week or more in Palo Alto and they were giving us all kinds of advice on places that would be fun for Allie to visit. They mentioned a couple of beaches they thought would be fun, Santa Cruz and Half Moon Bay. I didn't care; I just knew that we would have to find a way to get there. Allie's surgical nurse, Gina, had horses and offered to have us over for lunch and a chance to visit the horses. Everyone was so kind to us; they were all very attached to the little girl who had survived some terrible things. They were amazed by her strength and her smile and they were touched by our faith. We were discharged from the PICU before dinner. We were quite hungry and decided that spaghetti sounded good. I called my dad who left us all dinner at the front desk of the Ronald McDonald House before we even got there from the hospital. I was so grateful for warm food, a warm bed and no beeps or lights going off all night long. I was exhausted and was ready to put all of this behind us.

I had an uncle on my husband's side of the family who lived about two hours from Palo Alto. He wanted to take us to San Francisco for some seafood. I contacted him and he decided to come get us for a trip to the city on Sunday. That was perfect, as it gave us a day just to do nothing but rest and relax. Uncle Galen arrived and we borrowed a car seat for Allie for the trip. We were excited to get to do some sightseeing. Uncle Galen took us to Fisherman's Wharf and we had some of the best seafood we had ever eaten. We walked along the pier and looked for the sea lions and enjoyed our day. Uncle Galen was anxious to take us to Golden Gate Park. We loaded up and he got out his map. Uncle Galen, easily in his late 70's, was not able to see very well. This added some miles to our Golden Gate adventure. It was a blast, going up and down the streets of San Francisco looking for Golden Gate Park. Every now and then we would stop to ask directions, but we seemed to get nowhere closer to the park than when we started. It didn't matter to us though. Allie loved every second of the winding Lombard Street and couldn't quit saying "wheeee" with every roller coaster-like up and down of the hilly landscaped area. A couple of hours later, Uncle Galen threw in the towel. He was disappointed he hadn't found the park, but we had had so much fun just driving around. Uncle Galen was just one more angel making our trip to California more bearable and putting a smile on my baby girl's face. Allie didn't just smile with her mouth, her entire face lit up when she smiled and when she laughed, it was like hearing the angels sing in heaven.

Back at the house, we thanked Uncle Galen and he gave us his e-mail address so I could e-mail him the pictures I had taken that day. I took lots of pictures throughout the entire journey. Anytime I posted on Facebook about Allie's progress, I had to post a picture along with it. I knew, like most people know, that a picture can say it much better than my words can. I took anywhere from twenty to fifty pictures a day while we were there and deleted any that didn't live up to my standards.

I had been thinking about a trip to the beach and I had hatched a plan that just might work. Mom knew that my dad had "provided" some of the items in the room as well as some of the meals; she just didn't know that he was also the delivery man. As mother and I sat quietly reading our books in the room, while Allie watched a movie on the laptop, I began planting the seeds. "Mom," I said, "How do you think Chuck is able to get us the things he is getting for us? Do you really think he is giving a volunteer his credit card number and the volunteer is getting it for us?" I paused for an answer.

She answered, "Yes, I believe so . . . . why? What are you thinking?"

"I think he is here," I said innocently.

"What do you mean?" she said.

"I just think it is funny how quickly things get here and you know he really wanted to be here for Allie." I had her thinking now.

"That would really piss me off," she said.

I said, "Well think about it, he hasn't been bothering us. He has only been helpful. And now that her procedures are over, I think I will ask him if he is here and if he is, could he take us to a beach." I always referred to my dad as Chuck in front of my mother. My father's name is Charles, which is what my mother called him while they were married. After my father's second marriage, he became "Chuck". I called him "Chuck" in front of my mother because she made it clear on numerous occasions that she hated when I called him dad. Plus, the whole craziness of the two dads incident didn't help my situation. The children made it easier to call them "Grandpa Chuck" and "Grandpa Ken", thus differentiating between my two dads without hurting anybody's feelings.

Mom totally bought into the plan. I acted like I didn't know he was here, but that if he was here, we should ask him to take us to the beach. Mom said, "You make sure if he is here that he takes us to the airport on Friday as well." Of course, I knew my dad would be more than happy to do that, but I went along with mother. I excused myself to the hallway and told my dad what I had done.

He laughed and said, "Of course I would love to take all of you to the beach, out to dinner and by all means I will drive you all to the airport." It was instant relief. Everyone knew that everyone was there and no one was mad at me about it. I had seemingly escaped what could have been a very ugly scene; a scene that could have required a continuation of the charade and denied my courageous daughter the opportunity to visit a beach. There was no way Allie boarded that plane in Oklahoma thinking she was going to be in terrible pain and starved with IV's stuck in her the entire trip. She was under the complete impression that she was going to California to go to a beach. I was so happy, that she was going to get her wish.

We were scheduled to see Dr. Steinberg for a post-surgery appointment on Thursday and were due to fly back home on Friday. We decided we would schedule a trip to the beach on Tuesday. Monday was a day to relax and unwind from our trip to San Francisco with Uncle Galen. Allie's sutures were covered with glue on the most recent side of her surgery. The surgical nurse decided that it would be better to glue over the site than to put tape and gauze over it this time. The post-surgery tape and gauze removal was a screaming torture for Allie. Hair and suture covered with surgical tape had to be removed soon after surgery when the wound was still fresh and her headache was intense. The glue, we believed, would wear off gradually; ridding us of the screams of pain heard when we tore the tape off. The glue did rid us of the scream. But without the air getting to the wound, her sutures began to smell bad. They looked bad too. We contacted Dr. Steinberg's office on Monday and they told us to put Neosporin on it. This normally would have been very difficult to do. But since mom knew that my dad was here, I just called dad and had him take me to Target for supplies. It was a tremendous relief to be able to stop the dishonesty and the sneaking around. We would get to go to the beach and Allie would finally get to enjoy part of her trip to California.

Tuesday morning came and my dad met us in front of the Ronald McDonald House. He was taking us to Santa Cruz Beach. Santa Cruz Beach had a boardwalk with games and rides and all kinds of concessions. Allie was not able to ride any rides, of course, but she could play a mean one-armed game of putt-putt golf. She loved to play putt-putt golf, and the boardwalk just happened to have an indoor putt-putt course. We drove over an hour to our beach destination. I sat in front with dad driving and mom and Allie were in the back seat. I believe this was the first time that my two parents had been in a car together since the divorce. It was extremely awkward to say the least, but everyone was quietly civil to each other. We arrived at the beach and my dad had prepared blankets, cups and shovels for Allie to enjoy the sand. We immediately walked straight to the water and Allie's joy was evident in every part of her body. She could not physically wipe the smile off of her face. Every time the waves would hit her knees, she would squeal with joy and laugh herself silly. She kept saying, "Mom, look there's another one coming!" My eyes filled with tears of joy and I immediately knew that I had done the right thing. The smile on my baby's face was worth every possible repercussion of my deception. The water was cold, bone chilling cold. It was February and we were in the Bay area where the temperature is always a little cooler and the water is always cold. My mother wore jeans and a sweatshirt and my dad had his jacket and swim shorts on. I wore shorts with a jacket, as I rarely ever get too cold. We were able to stay and enjoy the waves for a very long time before Allie decided she wanted to look for sea shells. Before long, my mother had retreated to the benches on the boardwalk and my dad and Allie were hand in hand walking along the beach looking for shells. I left the beach to check on my mom's mental state. I refused to let anything interfere with the fun that Allie was having. I was relieved to find mother quietly sitting and enjoying herself, but not angry, at least, I didn't notice that she was angry. I walked back to the blanket and called the boys at school. The boys had never been to the beach and neither had Emma. I called the school office and asked that my three children be brought there so that I could talk to them. I spoke with each one in turn and faced the phone toward the waves going in and out so that they could hear what I heard. Each time I asked, "Where do you think I am?"

I would hold the phone close to the waves and turn it back to me and each child answered excitedly, "The beach! You are at the beach. No fair!" I told them how well Allie was doing and that they could mark the calendar for us to be home on Friday. I hadn't seen my family in over three weeks. It was a very long and stressful three weeks, and I couldn't wait to get back home. Allie and my dad made it back from their walk with a plastic grocery bag full of rocks and shells that Allie had collected. My dad then showed Allie all of the shovels and cups and helped her build a sand castle. She was having the time of her life. My dad went to the concessions and got us a souvenir cup filled with Dr. Pepper and a couple of corn dogs. Allie absolutely loved it. She could easily become a beach bum. All the time she spent in the hospital, all the needles and going without food, finally she was able to enjoy herself.

Finally, the cool temperatures got to Allie and although she protested leaving, she was covered in chill bumps and shivering all over. We went inside the boardwalk to use the restrooms and there it was . . . . a putt-putt golf course. Allie asked if she could play and of course, my dad splurged and let us all play! Mom sat back and just held our things for us while we played. Little did I know, with each passing moment, mom was getting more irritated. I was just enjoying watching Allie have fun! We didn't keep score, we just tried to make sure we didn't hold anyone up who was behind us. It took Allie several strokes to finish with that left arm swinging away, but she just had to finish. She refused to just call it at six strokes. At the end of the game, we left there tired and hungry, but happy. We decided to eat at our favorite place, the Olive Garden in Palo Alto. It would be another hour before we ate dinner, but it would be worth it. Having my mom and dad in the same vehicle going to the same beach and then to the same restaurant was awkward. At my wedding they avoided each other, at my high school graduation they sat on opposite sides of the gym. I had never seen them in close proximity to one another ever. At the restaurant they were cordial to each other, at best. Mom was quiet but she seemed to be taking it in stride. The dinner was amazing and my dad was gracious enough to pick up the check. Things seemed to be going very well actually and I was so grateful that everyone was keeping it together for Allie. We made it back to the Ronald McDonald House with a full day of memories and pictures, of course, that neither I nor Allie would ever forget.

We took that next day just to relax again. We didn't want Allie to get too tired from all of the activity. We needed her to rest on Wednesday and get ready to see the Doctor on Thursday. We were really praying that he would release us to fly home on Friday. Allie was doing really well. I was amazed at how alert she was after having brain surgery less than a week previously. The people at the Ronald McDonald House were also shocked when we told them what she was here for. They kept saying that she looked so good! She did, she was a precious girl who had amazing resolve and there wasn't much that would keep her down. We watched TV in the family room and went outside to play on the playground. We took a walk down by the creek that ran behind the Ronald McDonald House and just enjoyed the absolutely outstanding weather that Palo Alto provides. We were ready to go home, all of us and our families were ready for us to come home. We went to bed that evening anxiously awaiting the release from the Doctor so we could go home.

Thursday morning we woke up and went to the kitchen at the Ronald McDonald House. The electricity at the house was out but we were still able to get cereal from the pantry. The house had a common refrigerator where they kept milk and other staple items that anyone could use. They also had a pantry that served the same purpose. Cereal and milk were always available for breakfast, complements of the Ronald McDonald House. We ate our breakfast and caught a ride on the shuttle to the Stanford University Hospital where Doctor Steinberg's office is located. We didn't notice anything out of the ordinary until we arrived at the hospital. The electricity was out at the hospital as well as the Ronald McDonald House. Doctor Steinberg's office was on the third floor of the hospital and of course, with the electricity being out, the elevators were not running with the exception of the service elevators which were limited to hospital personnel or those with wheelchairs. We walked to the information desk at the hospital and asked if there was a way we could get to the third floor besides the elevators. They pointed us to the stairs and Allie and I were ready to go. Immediately mother pointed out that Allie had brain surgery a week earlier and should not be walking up and down three flights of stairs. My mother convinced them that we needed special assistance and they brought her a wheelchair. She climbed into the wheel chair and put Allie on her lap and I pushed the two of them onto the nearest service elevator. I wasn't exactly happy about that for a couple of reasons. I knew that Allie could have handled the stairs and I knew if we paced ourselves that my mother could have done them as well. I also knew that I had been through a lot during the last three weeks and that seeing the end nearing, my patience was wearing thin. The look on my face was best hidden behind my chair riders as I pushed the duo all the way across the building to the nearest service elevator. We arrived at the doctor's office and of course, their computers were having difficulty due to the power outage. Apparently, all of Palo Alto was out of power because a single engine airplane had crashed into a transformer. People were unable to get a cooked meal in town because all the restaurants had closed due to the lack of power. We had our visit in dim lighting and our sweet nurse handwrote as much as she could before she was able to get a signal on a battery operated computer. The rest of our visit was handled in the hallway, the only part of the office that had good internet access. God was once again good to us and we were released to go home the next day. We had a note in our hands for her return to school on Monday, as well as all of her recent films on disk in case something else happened. We also had notes that would keep her out of PE and athletics for the next two weeks. We were ready to go home. Our understanding was that the power was to remain off for the rest of the day because of all the damage to the transformer. We caught the shuttle back to the Ronald McDonald House and dug around in the pantry to find something that did not require power to eat. I called my dad to give him the good news of our release and we set a time for him to come and get us for the airport in the morning. He asked if he could take us to breakfast in the morning and I happily agreed. We all welcomed a good breakfast before we arrived at the airport. I thanked my dad and gave him a hug before leaving. He had done an amazing thing, in my eyes. He was helpful and there was an unspoken temporary truce between him and my mom during the last three weeks and for that I was extremely grateful.

We arrived in Tulsa very late and were elated to see our family there waiting for us. My mother-in-law, father-in-law, Donald, Brennan, Adam and Emma were there waiting. As soon as Allie saw them she ran straight full speed ahead into Brennan's arms. I could see the tears in Brennan's eyes as he was so grateful that we were home safe. His tears made me cry and I was embraced by Adam and Emma, both of whom would not let go of me. I held and carried Emma to get our luggage and Adam didn't leave my side. I gave a hug to everyone there and gave a quick kiss to my husband. Allie was so happy to be home. We didn't have much luggage to bring back, thanks to my dad. My dad's car was filled to the brim with things that we had acquired since our stay there. We were flying an airline that charged $20.00 per bag and would have well exceeded five bags, had we chosen to check it. My dad graciously offered to house it until he came up to visit us on Spring Break. Again, I was extremely grateful; he not only saved us money on luggage fees but also allowed us to take home all of the things we had gotten from people during our stay. We were finally home and our experience was behind us. I had learned long ago, not to get too excited about the prognosis, but I was definitely cautiously optimistic.

> *Be strong and courageous. Do not be terrified; do not be discouraged, for the Lord your God will be with you wherever you go. Joshua 1:9*

CHAPTER 22

We were back to school on Monday and things were getting back to normal for all of us. We were so grateful that it was all behind us and we were looking forward to summer break this year which was only three months away. No more hospitals for a while, no more surgeries. Life would be much less stressful and much more regular. But one troubling area still lingered from our trip to California; one more stress I knew had to be face.

After my step-dad, Ken, died in January of 2007, I'd made a promise to myself that I would call or text message mom every day. I had also given my mom our little dog "Bit", in the hopes that it would keep her company in that house all by herself. I felt responsible for keeping her happy, for making sure that she didn't get lonely after Papa Ken died. I also called her on the weekends to see if she needed anything from the store, or wanted to go shopping with me and a couple of the kids. I knew she wasn't a big fan of having all the kids with us, it stressed her out. So, I tried to take only one or two with us on our outings. My sister and I made a special effort to take her out for lobster on her and daddy's anniversary. She loved lobster and she and daddy went every year on their anniversary to get it. It was very hard on my mom being by herself. She and daddy went everywhere together. They didn't need any friends from church or anything, they had each other. So when daddy (aka, Papa Ken) died, I made every effort to include her in my days. We went to lunch or I invited her to our church. I invited her to dinner whenever I thought of it but I took great care to make sure that she didn't get too lonely. She even let me take her credit card and decorate her house. I loved decorating and painting her house. I especially loved those rub-on sayings that were both biblical and inspirational. After school started, I became super busy and wasn't as able to do things with her. I did call or text every day though, I rarely missed a day. I noticed however, that after our trip to California, she wasn't texting me or picking up my calls. I wondered if she had found out that I knew my dad was there all along. It was the only explanation I could think of that she would stop speaking to me entirely. I cornered her into going shopping with me in nearby Owasso. I knew in my heart that she had something pressing to discuss with me. I asked her if she was upset with me about something, and out it came. She started about how she was thinking that I knew that my dad was there all along and that she was upset that I would lie to her about it. I was caught. I was relieved though, I hated lying and keeping secrets. I knew eventually it would have to come out. I confessed and apologized profusely for my deception. She said, "You are not a very nice person."

I said, "No, I am probably not." I told her to try to see it from my point of view. I reminded her of how I told him not to come and that he specifically decided on his own to come anyway. She did not understand. She was angry, so angry she was crying. I just kept apologizing. I didn't know what else to say. I was exhausted. I began to pray during the silence of the ride to Owasso that she would find it in her heart to forgive me. I didn't want her to be so mad that she refused to be in our lives. God intervened on my behalf again, and somehow her anger was focused solely on my father. We were able to finish our shopping trip and I took her out to lunch. It was out and she wasn't too mad at me and we were able to do things together again. It was another answer to a prayer, another blessing from God.

Our summer continued uneventful except for the occasional short lived TIA. Allie and Emma were in speech therapy and Allie continued to receive Physical Therapy at Claremore Regional Hospital. I also took the four children to the Library in Claremore. They all got their library cards and checked out books frequently. Brennan was taking guitar lessons and Adam was very interested in sleeping past noon daily. I didn't mind that too much but I didn't like him sleeping until later in the afternoon. That seemed to be a problem especially on Sundays when we were trying to get to church. There were probably a lot of things going on in their little heads that I didn't even know about that summer. No one seemed to know when or if Allie would relapse and it seemed we were always very cautious about planning anything too far in advance. Brennan and Adam seemed to be particularly affected. They seemed to fight more and more. The more they fought, the later Adam would sleep in. The door to the girl's room, with the exception of one bathroom, was the only room that had a lock on the door. Adam began playing with his Lego's behind the locked door throughout the night, and would sleep until 5:00 p.m. behind the locked door. This presented several problems, not the least of which was he had his days and nights mixed up. One morning I woke up around 8:00 a.m. and noticed that Adam was almost "hyper awake", babbling incessantly with his eyes weirdly wide open. I was instantly worried. I knew this was not normal. I had heard about infants getting their days and nights mixed up, but not a nine year old. I contacted a developmental pediatrician and told her we were in crisis. She was able to get us in almost immediately. Adam spent almost 45 minutes in her office answering her questions and talking about Legos. She gave him three wishes and asked him to tell her about them. I was in the other room, where I could hear him respond. He said his first wish would be that he could have the entire Lego City Collection. He told the doctor exactly how he could order it online and many other tidbits of Lego information, just in case she was interested. Adam's second wish was that he would like to eat spaghetti. He began telling her about a time when he was little that he enjoyed eating spaghetti with red sauce. He told her, he no longer had a taste for it and it was something the entire family ate together. He wished he liked it again so he could sit at the table with us and eat it. His third wish was that he could have his own room. Adam desperately needed and wanted his own room. We were stuck with a house that had only three bedrooms. One was mine and Donald's, one was the girls' and one the boys'. He and Brennan got along so poorly, that Adam refused to sleep in his and Brennan's room. Because the girls slept with me at night, Adam had decided to use their room as his own. He hated the pink and purple of the room, but he loved the lock on the door. He felt safe in there during the day and at night. He felt safe from Brennan and his teasing, safe from the girls taking his Lego's or accidentally breaking one of his creations. He was very protective of his creations and would fly into a rage if anyone touched them. He also had collections of feathers, rocks, cars, and trains that no one else was allowed to touch. I agreed with him, he did need his own room. It was difficult to sort out though with the lack of space and his need to be by himself so much.

The doctor finished her interview and Adam and I switched rooms. I asked her what her professional opinion was. She said, "He definitely has high-functioning autism." I knew it; in my heart I knew it. He was always just a little quirky and a loner. He obsessed over trains until the age of seven at which time he switched over to an obsession for Legos. Everything I had feared was confirmed about my little boy. She offered to give him a prescription for a sleep aid and I assured her, he wouldn't take it. She brought him in and asked him if he would take it and for her, he promised to. I went home with Adam's prescription and just reflected on my life. My Brennan, who I loved with all my heart and soul, was going to be battling a lifetime of Attention Deficit Disorder. My Emma who was extremely small for her age, I loved with all my heart. My Allie, with all of her brain damage and TIA activity, was wandering the planet literally, noticing the bright yellow hue of a flower or the feel of the wall as she dragged her left hand along it, keeping her right hand tight to her side. My Adam, who I also loved with all of my heart and soul, would be trying to fit in socially to this world. He would have to overcome his difficulty with social interaction. It didn't change who Adam was, it just gave a name to what he had.

I sat with my letter that announced his diagnosis to the school, not quite ready for the world to know. I was sure the school personnel and his teachers likely already knew this about him. If I suspected it, I was sure they did. I took the rest of the day off from things around the house and just enjoyed Adam. He loved to snuggle and for that I was extremely grateful. We picked out a DVD to watch, he crawled up beside me and allowed me to hold him the rest of the day. I came to peace with what God had given me that day. I knew that however different our lives were from most others that we were blessed. We didn't get caught up in silly things like designer clothes or big houses or having ridiculous things. We had our own set of things that we thought about during the day, none of them had anything to do with "things." We knew what was important in life. We had God, we had each other and we had a future of enjoying the blessings that God had provided us.

> *Do not store up for yourselves treasures on earth, where moth and rust destroy, and where thieves break in and steal. But store up for yourselves treasures in heaven, where moth and rust do not destroy, and where thieves do not break in and steal. For where your treasure is, there your heart will be also. Matthew 6:19-21*

CHAPTER 23

꽃

We were scheduled to go back to Stanford at the beginning of August for a re-check. Because we were lucky enough for her six month follow-up to fall before school restarted, we decided to take the entire family. We hadn't really ever been on a family vacation for that long, so far from home. Allie called it "her" California, "her" beach, and "her" hospital. That definitely annoyed the other three, but they went along with it since it meant they would get to see a beach in California.

That summer I was very intent on getting my room ready before we left for California. I knew that our return would be very near to the time I would have to report. Brennan had gone out for football and during his practices I would go up and work on my room. I spent hours in the room, knowing I needed to be ready to go before I left for California. I didn't need any other stress if I was to support to my daughter while she got all of her follow-up tests there at Stanford.

I woke up one Sunday morning and was in excruciating pain. I had pinched a nerve in my shoulder. I made an appointment with my friend who is a masseuse. An hour later saw no difference. My left arm was in terrible pain constantly and my hand and fingers were numb. I went to an after-hours care where they gave me a prescription painkiller. The painkiller certainly wiped out the pain, but once it wore off, I was right back where I started. I was thankful that I had finished everything I needed to in my classroom; or so I thought. About week before we went on vacation, our superintendent, decided to have new tile put into the rooms down our hallway. I had no idea exactly what it meant until I went up to take a look at it myself. My room was a disaster. They had moved everything off of the tile and piled it onto the carpet part of the room. Paper was everywhere and somehow my fish had died during the move. One of the cabinet doors was broken off at the top and hung crooked on the cabinet face. All of the money I had spent on these things, all of the time I had spent getting everything ready set in on me and I began to cry. Defeated, I left the room and vowed that I would not worry about it until after we were home from the hospital in California. I was determined not to let it ruin our trip. My arm, however, was a different story. I decided to get an appointment with my regular Doctor and was relieved when he prescribed me an anti-inflammatory and a steroid. I felt much better instantly. My arm would start out in pain in the morning, but after I took my medicine, it actually felt a lot better. We drove to the airport in early August, all four children and husband together for our trip to California.

We hadn't really been on a vacation before with all six of us, so we weren't sure what to expect. It took a lot of planning on our part. Many of the hotels would only allow four people to stay in a room. Rental cars are much more expensive and fewer in number if they hold more than five people. We got the cheapest flights we could get but those cheap flights mean that seats were not guaranteed. The business travelers get the aisle seats so they can exit quickly and stick their legs into the aisle. I thought I would save the business travelers the stress and we boarded as a family during pre-boarding with the other families with small children. The flight itself was fun as I got to watch the faces of my children light up as the plane took off. They loved every minute of the flight. Adam was quite nervous during his first take-off and had a look on his face of terror until we were safely in the air. We arrived at the San Jose airport and went straight to our rental van. The air was perfect, sixty-five degrees and my children could not get over how wonderful the temperatures in California were in August. In Oklahoma, we don't generally see a day below 100 in the month of August. It was a relief to be on the ground and headed to our hotel. The hotel was perfect for us; it had a swimming pool, laundry services, free breakfast and two queen beds. We settled in, the kids got their swimsuits on and jumped into the pool. Allie could have nothing to eat after midnight as her first round of tests that required anesthesia began early the next morning with check in at the Ford Family Surgery Center. I was appointed to go with Allie on Monday and I was hopeful that Donald would take the kids sightseeing around Palo Alto while we were at the hospital. I decided that Donald would go on Tuesday during her flow study as this was the least invasive and shortest of the tests. Monday was her arteriogram which required the scope that went up through her leg and into her brain to check for arteries that had developed post-surgery that were supplying blood to her brain. The arteriogram took the longest and required a six hour stay in the short stay unit of the hospital. The last time we were there, we ended up spending the night because she spiked a fever. I was praying that this time, it would be completely uneventful and we would be able to go to the hotel directly after. I was far too acquainted to what were really very dangerous procedures. Most parents would be a mess going into such a procedure on their child. I had been through six arteriograms and I had been completely blessed with no complications. God had been so good to us and I was so grateful that He was watching out for Allie during all of her procedures. I was a little nervous, but nothing that would compare to how I felt before an actual brain surgery.

Allie and I woke early before anyone and dressed for the hospital. Once there, we immediately headed for the Ford Family Surgery Center. I knew it was going to be a long day, but I continued to be optimistic that it would go smoothly and we would be out of the hospital before dark. Things were moving slowly and our arteriogram was delayed, but not by much. We were on our way within a couple of hours. She woke up an hour and a half after her procedure in recovery, already asking for something to eat. We went through the usual steps to get to eat real food and we were released to the short stay unit so she could keep her leg straight for the next six hours. In the short stay unit, the nurse immediately ordered Allie something to eat from the cafeteria. We watched television and I called Donald to see how the kids were doing. Donald said the kids were having fun swimming in the pool and just enjoying a relaxing day at the hotel. We were blessed once more, as six hours from the completion of her procedure Allie was released from the hospital to go back to the hotel. Donald and the kids came to pick us up and we had dinner out at a local Mexican restaurant in Palo Alto.

Tuesday morning, we took Donald and Allie to the hospital. We dropped them off so the rest of us could have the car for the day. I took Brennan, Adam and Emma to the Stanford Shopping Mall. There were beautiful flowers and wishing wells and of course McDonald's for lunch. The weather was just so beautiful; we had so much fun just walking around together. We waited for Donald to call and tell us to come and pick them up. I talked Donald into taking the kids to Muir Woods while I took Allie to her MRI on Wednesday. The kids seemed to really have a good time and they came back with all kinds of souvenirs. Allie was unhappy when we got back to the hotel and she realized she had missed out on a fun trip. We redeemed ourselves, the next day by taking everyone to the beach after the Doctor's appointment.

We were again, extremely blessed and grateful when Dr. Steinberg gave us the results of the tests. He was impressed by all of the collateral blood flow she had already developed in her brain since the surgery. From what he could tell, she was adequately revascularized and wouldn't need to see us again for three years. "Three years"; those words just kept going over and over again in my head. I did the math in my head, Brennan would be fifteen, Adam would be twelve and the girls would be nine. Could this mean that we could be in the clear for the next three years? Could we really be out of the woods in regard to an upcoming debilitating stroke? Had God really given us such a gift that our little girl might be able to get on with her life without having to do this all over again for the next three years? Words cannot express how absolutely happy and relieved I felt. We headed out for the Santa Cruz Beach Boardwalk that very day, completely happy with the news we had been given at the Doctor's office.

We arrived at the Santa Cruz Beach Boardwalk and the excitement in the car was tangible. The other three had never been to a beach before and so they couldn't wait to get onto the sand. They were almost impossible to contain. We arrived on the beach and set up a spot to relax and play in the sand. Adam took immediately to building a sand castle. He used several cups and sticks along with some rocks and shells to make a castle that was hard to top. Brennan just rolled around in the sand and jumped the waves with as much happiness as we had ever seen. Allie and Emma spent most of the time in the water, jumping the waves, holding their nose and going under water and coming back up again. All four of the children absolutely loved playing at the beach. The air became quite chilly when the sun finally went down so we headed up to the boardwalk to get some nice thick hoodies. The girls were shivering and were covered in goose bumps. I am sure that none of us ever imagined that a beach would be so cold during the month of August, but it was very chilly. We were only able to hold out another hour after dark as we walked the lit boardwalk and just enjoyed each other's company. It was almost surreal that we were actually doing the things that normal families do for a change. Of course, we had endured an entire week of hospital and doctor visits, and painful IV's and tests, but we didn't have to go back for three years. I was very happy and I immediately gave God the glory and the thanks for all of the blessings He had given us.

We headed back home with barely enough time to get ourselves psyched up for school to start. I had to report that upcoming Thursday and it was difficult to adjust to the time change and adjust to not getting to sleep in. I made it up to my classroom the weekend we returned home and got my room ready for open-house. I was relieved that I was able to get it done. I wasn't completely sure I would the way I left it before we went to California. I was anxious to start school. I was getting excited about meeting all of my new kindergarten students and the girls were excited for their second year of kindergarten. Allie had missed so much of her first year of kindergarten from all of her surgeries and I just decided that one more year in kindergarten wouldn't hurt either of them one bit. Adam was entering third grade with a teacher that I knew for sure was going to be perfect for him. Brennan was back at our campus where I would get to see him every day. I was happy to have all of my kids at the same campus for the first time and the last time ever.

Brennan was entering the seventh grade and was preparing for football season. He was playing football for the first time ever and I was very nervous. Those football boys were huge and fearless and I was worried that my boy would get hurt under all those bigger boys. Football didn't last long, as Brennan missed playing his trumpet in the band. Personally, I think he noticed those bigger boys too, and he decided he'd better be safe than sorry. It didn't matter why he stopped playing, just that he had and he was back playing his trumpet not long after that. Before long, he had earned his first chair spot and he was easily making A's in every class. I was so proud of him. Adam was doing well also and was reading above grade level. He was reading and consuming so many books that he had almost earned 150 accelerated reading points. Emma was doing amazingly well and was actually reading books to the class. It was as if for Emma, all of the sudden a switch flipped on and she could read books like never before. Allie was taking things a little slower, but she was making progress just the same. She seemed to be having a great time in her second year of kindergarten, but she was still very slow to process things. I was blessed to be able to see her on the playground every couple of days and I loved being able to watch both her and Emma play. I loved having my kids come to my room after school. I even had Adam cleaning the tables and stacking the chairs after school while I did my bus duties. It was going to be a great year. Our two seasoned teachers had left, one retired and the other now the computer teacher, so I was now the seasoned kindergarten teacher. My five years teaching kindergarten was more than the two new teachers who were first year kindergarten teachers. I was excited to take the lead and share all of the things I did with the children in my classroom. The year had the potential to be the best year ever. But as I had become all too familiar with, life's small victories can be short lived.

CHAPTER 24

Not long into the school year, the speech-pathologist wanted to pull the girls out for speech services during their direct phonics instruction time. I objected to this mostly because it was their last chance to get it, their last chance in kindergarten. I talked to their teacher and let her know that I did not want them pulled during the time she was doing her direct phonics teaching time. She agreed and said that she and the speech-pathologist would work it out. I was relieved when I knew that the girls' teacher was really looking out for them. Not long after I voiced my objection, the girls' teacher informed me that she and the speech-path decided it would be okay to pull them during direct instruction. I went to my principal and stated my concerns about them being pulled during that time and she thought it was a good idea if we had an IEP meeting; IEP—Individualized Education Plan. An IEP is in place on all students who have special needs and it states in writing all therapeutic services the child receives. I was a little hesitant, because I felt like I was fighting a losing battle, but I went along with it. I talked to Donald about it and told him that if he was in agreement with me that it was a bad idea to pull the girls for speech during direct instruction, that it would be beneficial if he attended the meeting and said so. He agreed and we all came together for our meeting. All it took was my husband, voicing his concerns about it for the speech-pathologist to find another time to see my girls. I was relieved and irritated at the same time. I just made a special effort for the rest of the semester to pray hard for those involved in that meeting. I knew that it would take God's grace and love for me to set aside the irritation I was feeling about them. It took a while, but I was finally able to let it go, again, another miracle that came from our precious Lord.

Just after spring break in 2011, Allie's teacher brought her to me and said, "Allie is slurring her speech, I think something is wrong." I was beyond the point of getting excited too easily because of everything we had been through. While still in class, I just had Allie lie down in the reading area while I continued to finish out the school day. I went to check on her around lunch time and found her to be running a fever. I decided that she must be sick and this is why she is having a TIA. I checked out and went home for the rest of the day. I was hoping that given the chance to rest, Allie would come out of this feeling better and the TIA's would stop. Allie slept most of the afternoon but after dinner, she had another one. Her speech was extremely slurred and her arms and legs went limp. I dragged her to the bed and began to panic a little. I timed the TIA at just less than eleven minutes. It subsided though and we were able to go on with our evening. An hour later, Brennan came running to me screaming "She's having another one mom, something is wrong with her." He was obviously panicked and I was becoming more panicked. She hadn't had that many TIA's in one day since her stroke and I was beginning to wonder if she was having another stroke. I called the neurologist in Tulsa who told me to take her to the emergency room. Before we left for the hospital, she had had another one. It seemed as if with each one, she didn't quite fully recover, never quite returned to baseline. I called my mother and had her stay with the kids as Donald was working midnights. During the 45 minute drive to Tulsa, she had another one in her car seat.

I could hear her slurring her words as she said, "Mommy are there flowers in heaven?"

"I think so," I said.

"Mommy, I miss papa Ken," she said weakly.

I turned around and tearfully pleaded, "Not tonight Allie. You are not going to leave us tonight, you hang on." I prayed as I drove and listened to her carefully. We arrived at the hospital and I carried her limp body 500 feet to the door. I was winded and anxious as we checked in at the window. They knew we were coming as the neurologist had phoned ahead and told them what was going on. They immediately got us back and it was after midnight. Allie continued to have slurred speech and slowed thinking. I asked her several questions about pet's names and family names which took her minutes to answer so I knew she was still in the middle of a TIA. They told us that we were being admitted and that the neurologist wanted an MRI and CT scan to check for stroke. We were admitted to the PICU that evening and awoke the next morning to nothing by mouth until after her MRI. My head was spinning, I was a mess. I thought we were done with all of this; three years before California wanted to see us again. The doctors and nurses said she looked great. I could not understand what was going on, why all of the sudden she was going through this again. I went back with her to the MRI and the CT. In Tulsa, she didn't have to be sedated for either procedure, because they had the movie headphones for the MRI machine. I assumed the order of no food or drink was precautionary in case she had indeed suffered a stroke. I wasn't completely sure what their plan was for her. I knew that historically, there wasn't anything they could do for her here. I also knew that I had no desire to go to Texas or California again. Our three years weren't up; we weren't supposed to be here again. It was completely unacceptable and completely unbelievable. I immediately went to God. He knew I wasn't happy. He knew that I was tired, confused, and angry. I didn't have to tell Him, because He knew, but I told Him anyway. I also asked that He please help us once again. I begged Him to give us an end to these TIA's that were leaving my baby unable to speak, drink, swallow or purse her lips.

Allie continued her TIA's and was up to eleven in a 24 hour period. I was getting very irritated at the Doctor on-call. She was walking up and down the hall checking on other patients and she would send an intern in from time to time but I knew in my heart she had no answers for us. They still hadn't given her the okay to eat and it was nearing 4:00 in the afternoon. That of course meant that I hadn't eaten either and I get pretty grumpy when I am hungry. I started telling Allie to press the nurse button and I told her to tell them she was hungry. She did it a couple of times and each time, they insisted they would send the doctor in to talk to us. Finally, fed up, I went to the nurse and told her, "Listen, I understand that she is not allowed to eat until the MRI results are up. Do you have a plan for what you will do for her if she has had a stroke? If you do not have a plan, I don't understand the problem with letting her go ahead and have something to eat. Can you please just ask the doctor what her plan is if she has had a stroke?" The nurse went out and came back in with news that the MRI had shown no new strokes, and Allie could eat. She also stated that our neurologist would be coming in to talk to us some time tonight. I had planned to run home and shower and see the kids before seeing the neurologist, but there was no time now. I stayed, feeling hungry and tired and sick. I could tell I had thoroughly irritated the doctor as now, she and her interns would not even look our direction when they passed our room. It was all a part of the joys of being a mother and an advocate. The neurologist came in around 7:00 p.m. to tell us that there were no new strokes but that he wanted to keep her and run a continuous 48 hour EEG on her to check if these were seizures. We had been through all of that before, but I could not really object. I felt totally helpless. I knew in my heart these were not seizures. I was a little hopeful that they were because they actually had medication for that and it would explain all of this craziness.

I told the neurologist how I had apparently upset the staff and his response was, "Who cares?" He told me that it was my job to advocate for Allie and that there would be a new shift with new doctors and nurses the next day. I felt a lot better. He told me just to call him directly on his cell phone if anything like that happened again and he would take care of it for me. This doctor was a complete blessing to us. I am not sure what we would have done, or where we would have been without him. He also stated that although the nurses would likely object, he was keeping us in PICU to be monitored closely. He was afraid if he moved us to the floor and something happened, they would not get to us in time. I was okay with that but I was definitely hoping for new faces in the morning. I was looking forward to faces that weren't mad at me for throwing my fit yesterday about Allie's eating. At about midnight, the EEG tech came in to attach all of the electrodes to Allie's head. We had been down this road a couple of times before and I knew we were in for a nice aftermath of sticky glue in her hair for the next couple of weeks or so. I think Allie actually fell asleep while she was being hooked up to the EEG equipment and not long after that, I fell asleep as well.

The next morning showed promise as I didn't recognize any of our caretakers. There was a new doctor on call who was making rounds with new interns. They asked me to push the button if Allie had an episode so it could be marked on the EEG to be analyzed by the neurologist for seizure activity. It wasn't too difficult as I told Allie to tell me if she was getting ready to have one. She knew when they were coming and she would say, "Mommy my tongue feels funny." This gave me plenty of time to push the button and document the episode on the EEG. By the end of the day, I had logged three episodes on the EEG and was waiting for the neurologist to come in and tell us the results of the EEG. By that evening, the neurologist came by to confirm that the episodes logged onto the EEG showed no evidence of being seizures. I knew in my heart that the problems Allie was having were not seizures but I was happy that we had some answers at least. The neurologist wanted to leave the EEG equipment on her another twelve hours. In those twelve hours, I logged one last episode on the EEG. The neurologist called and confirmed that this also was not a seizure. All this time, our neurologist had been consulting with Stanford and Dr. Steinberg's office. He was taking his cues from them and consulting with them at every step. Dr. Steinberg wanted a flow study, something they didn't offer in Oklahoma. Our neurologist released us from the hospital but told me that I should contact Dr. Steinberg's office as soon as possible. Released on a Friday, I waited the weekend before I was able to contact Dr. Steinberg's office in California.

Allie's TIA activity had slowed dramatically but she was still having episodes, at least once a day. This was completely unheard of, as we had gone almost three months without any activity at all. I had a bad feeling that something was terribly wrong. I was worried about her vertebral arteries that supply blood to the back of the brain. The vertebral arteries were the only two large arteries she had left. I was praying that those were okay, if she lost either or both of those, Allie's fight for her life would be over.

On Monday morning, the first day of spring break, I called Dr. Steinberg's office in Palo Alto California. I left a message for Bob, the service coordinator and while I was leaving the message, Bob was calling me on my cell phone. He said that Dr. Steinberg wanted to see Allie and run some tests on her, specifically the tests that they were unable to run in Oklahoma. He asked what day was good for me. I laughed because it was not an easy thing to fly out, find housing and miss work to go out to California for a week. I told him that the current week was actually good, because we were on Spring Break; at that he laughed. Shortly after that call, Dr. Steinberg's nurse called to get more details. I said to her, "If there isn't anything you can do for her, we are not going to come all the way to California. We are only coming, if there is something you can do to help her." Dr. Steinberg's nurse assured me that there were a lot of options and several things they could do to help her. We settled on the week after Spring Break and at this point I had some decisions to make.

Grandpa Chuck, dad, was up from Austin visiting and he offered to drive to Palo Alto, pick us up at the airport and give us a place to stay while we were there. My mom was also offering to pay our airfare and hotel so that we wouldn't have to stay with my dad. She wanted to go but she had made it very clear that she was not going again after the deception of the previous trip. I know it didn't bother mom to pay our way down, but we had been given so much for so long and my dad's offer didn't involve putting anyone out. I was terrified that I would upset my mother, but I had to accept my dad's offer. A car to take us where we needed to be and a place to stay for free took a lot of my stress away, so I graciously accepted my dad's offer. He left the next day to start driving down so he could be there when we got there on Sunday. I called my mom and as I predicted she was upset. She did insist on paying our airfare which was a huge help. Thanks be to God as He is good to us all the time.

We were preparing to leave for California in four days and my children were completely distraught. Emma was crying most days and would not let me out of her sight. She was begging to go with us and crying. It was all I could do to not buy her a ticket and pay the consequences of that decision later. I knew though that the tests they would run would require me to be there with Allie and Emma would not be allowed in the room. This would put another separation between us and a complete breakdown with kicking and screaming at the hospital or worse, at my dad's motor home. I tried to comfort her as best I could but honestly, I was growing very tired. I was sick and tired of having to jump on an airplane and leave my other children in the hands of numerous friends and relatives. I was sick and tired of seeing people stick needles in my daughter's arm and deprive her of food for hours on end. I was sick and tired of watching my other kids cry for me, beg me to stay and smother me, never letting me get out of their sight. I was not in good shape. I knew my mother was mad because she refused to answer my calls or texts. The last thing I needed was my mother throwing a fit because I was staying at my dad's motor home. I needed to be in prayer 24 hours a day with the things I had on my plate. Donald was irritated because he was going to have to take a couple of days off to be at home while the floor installers were putting in our new floor. What I really wanted to do was sleep, go to sleep for a couple of days and wake up with all of this being a dream. Unfortunately the kids had broken my bed jumping on it and it was being propped up with chairs. The bed was still uneven and I found myself sliding to the southwest corner of the room on the bed during the night. I was not getting good sleep and I was getting ready to fly to California. I hadn't planned on being gone and so I had nothing ready for a substitute teacher at school. I tried to get a few things ready for the next week. I am not sure where I got the time frame of a week, but I'd convinced myself that I would be back in a week. God had other plans.

I realized that I needed to reduce the little things on the trip that caused me great stress. The first of those things was making sure to fly an airline where we had reserved seats. One silver lining about our situation was that I had become a seasoned traveler. We carried only one bag on and sent the remainder of our luggage with my dad in the motor home. Once again, I convinced Allie that we were going to California to swim at the beach. It was March and terribly cool in Oklahoma, but I knew the weather in California stayed pretty much the same throughout the year. Our flights were uneventful and we were able to roam around at the DFW airport and slowly reach our connecting gate. We had to go to the entire other end of the airport to catch our connecting flight and had to ride the "train". Allie loved riding the train. She would squeal "wheeeee" when we were on it. Dad picked us up at the airport and the air was absolutely perfect. He drove us to the motor home and we settled in as best we could. We were very thankful for a place to stay and dad took us out to dinner at Allie's favorite Italian restaurant, where she ordered spaghetti. We knew the next day would start a round of craziness beginning with another arteriogram to measure blood flow in her brain. Allie continued to have TIA's but they were limited to only two a day at most. Two a day, however, was more than we were used to and I was relieved to finally be here where they could actually do something for her. I always disliked the trip to California, but I always felt better once we were there.

Monday morning, we headed to check in at the Ford Family Surgery Center. The people had begun to recognize us and knew our names we had been there so often. We got there at 6:30 a.m. for our 6:45 check-in and found the door locked. They weren't quite open yet but as we stood there, they opened the door for us. As we pushed the door open, the fire alarm went off. It was the first time I had heard the fire alarm at the hospital. We got to hear it several times at the Ronald McDonald House but never at the hospital. It was loud and resounding and we shut the door behind us to block the sound. We asked if this was a drill to which no one at the desk knew the answer. After about 20 minutes, the alarm subsided and we went back to business as usual. I reflected for a little while on what an evacuation of the hospital would mean for us and how far back her arteriogram would be pushed and how much longer she would have to go without eating. Thankfully, things were moving quite smoothly that day and her arteriogram began as scheduled. I instantly thanked God for the blessing of having procedures on-time and asked that He keep His protective hand on Allie. Dad and I retreated for the cafeteria and breakfast. My dad told me at that time, that he had been instructed by my step-mother that I was not to pay for any food. He and my step-mother had decided that they would buy all our meals while we were here. Again, God was taking very good care of us through the love of friends and family. I'm not sure what we would have done throughout this entire experience without friends and family who loved us so much, that they saw fit to take care of our every need. Even as my dad and I were eating breakfast, two very good friends of mine, Dawna and Lora were in Oklahoma going furniture shopping to get me a new bed. They knew about my current bed being held up by chairs and they also knew that with children and animals sleeping with me that I was in desperate need of a king size bed. They also knew that if they didn't take care of things while I was gone, that I may have been without a decent bed for months to come. It was no coincidence that I had been asking for a king size bed since the girls were born. We had angels looking out for us in every direction. I had even been in contact with Allie's surgical nurse who wanted to take us out to lunch while we were in town.

Allie's procedure went without incident and we were sent from recovery to short-stay unit very quickly. Again, I was hoping beyond hope, that we would be released in a timely fashion and was again praying that God would help us to get out of there as soon as we were able. I still didn't like hospitals and I felt like we had spent the better part of the last two years in them. I knew that if I didn't like hospitals, Allie probably disliked them even more. She was always so easy going. As long as they provided her with food and a television, she was a great sport about all of it. Again, in an answer to prayer, we were released six hours past the ending of her arteriogram and my dad drove us back to the motor home. We were so anxious and excited to find out what the arteriogram showed. We were all looking forward to meeting with Dr. Steinberg. I still worried that one of her vertebral arteries was dissecting but felt some relief that her condition hadn't really gotten any worse in the last week. I was sure that if one of those arteries was dissecting, we would see it in her immediately and she would be declining quite rapidly. This gave me some peace of mind.

We arrived at Dr. Steinberg's office about thirty minutes before our appointment time. My dad, being in the military, was always early for everything. We checked in and were able to see Dr. Steinberg right at our appointment time. Dr. Steinberg pulled up the scans from the arteriogram and began to speak. He said that clearly she did not have enough blood flow to the regions of her brain on the upper left side. He could see that she was fully revascularized in the other areas from the surgeries he had performed. He said, "I have done over 800 of these surgeries and have only had to redo three of them. It looks like she may need to be number four."

I looked at him and said, "Seriously? I am just about sick and tired of being so rare and special." He laughed a little but said it was my call. He would do the surgery while we were there or we could wait and see if the TIA's diminished. I didn't even hesitate. I knew that God was with us and I said, "Just do it now. We are here now and it is incomprehensible to imagine her learning anything in school if her brain is going to sleep every four hours or so." He instantly started going over his schedule and found a spot for Allie on Thursday, a week later. I called the surgical nurse and she assured me that she was on the calendar that day, and she would be in there with Allie the entire time. Because he had to work us in however, her surgery would be in the afternoon and she could have nothing by mouth before the surgery, again. We had a week to do some things that Allie wanted to do. I had a week to get myself ready for this nightmare again. We were also scheduled for an MRI on Monday, flow studies on Tuesday and blood drawn in preparation for the surgery on Thursday. This was not in the three year plan.

We went out to lunch and I began mental preparation for what was to come. I had complete confidence in Dr. Steinberg; I just dreaded the hospital stay. The last time she had surgery here was unbearable, terrifying and not at all family friendly. I had written a five page letter to the administration of the hospital spelling out for them the areas in which they could improve. They had responded to my letter with gratitude and the promise of changes. I was very quiet, as I usually am when I am deep in thought and my dad asked me if I was okay. I was stressed about the next couple of weeks. I was stressed about leaving the children in my classroom with a substitute teacher. I was worried about my children and who was taking care of them when Donald was at work. I was still not getting any thing from my mom, no answer to texts, and no phone calls. I prayed about it and continued to text her every day to let her know how Allie was doing; every text went unanswered. More than anything, I was worried about Allie; another hospital stay in PICU without eating again. She seemed tired. Her resolve and patience were fleeting. I was again on my knees praying for strength for both of us. I posted on Facebook for prayers for us. We were feeling the weight of the world again on our shoulders and it was up to the both of us to stay upbeat, positive and continue to hope for the best despite our apparent odds at being rare and special.

At this point, we began running low on snacks and we took a much needed trip to a local Target store. Allie and I loved to shop and it was a much needed boost for our mood. We were getting close to Easter and our absolute favorite mini-eggs were available for purchase as well our other personal favorite, marshmallow peeps. For some reason, a trip to Target made us feel normal, like one of any of the other shoppers, just there for a trip to the store. It was just what we needed as we headed back to the motor home to let everyone know what was going on.

I called the school to let them know I would be gone for another two weeks or so. I was again completely out of sick leave and I just assumed that I would be off without pay. One of the most generous things that had been done for me during every one of these hospital stays was the donation of leave time people gave me every time I was out. I would start the year with the ten sick days that all teachers get but would easily be out if there were any trips to the hospital at all. I ran out every year since Allie's stroke and every year, my colleagues and friends would donate leave time to me. It was one of the most generous things I had ever seen. As much as I wanted to thank each and every person who donated, the individuals who donated remained clouded in confidentiality. I couldn't find out who did it even if I wanted to. I knew there were a few in my general circle of friends who likely donated, but only being able to donate three days a year, it would take way more than just four or five people to cover me. At this point, I felt like I was constantly a burden to people. So many people had given us money, my dad was buying our meals, mom paid our airfare, the church had collected more than $2,000 for us, RCB Bank had established an account for us that also had thousands of dollars donated; I felt like it was too much. We of course, needed the money and used every penny to get us to and from California all the times that we had been. In fact, I had closed out the account before this last trip to California for copayments or medicines and other things we might need while we were there. I had no idea that through so many people's compassion and generosity that I would never miss a day's pay and that our trips would be virtually paid for through the giving of others. Again, God had blessed us beyond belief. I was beginning to worry though, that people were sick of me using their leave, that people were tired of hearing about all of our medical problems and I didn't want one more day to be donated by my friends. I wanted it to be my turn to give back to them. I wanted to be the one to do for others, to donate money or leave or just bring dinner to someone whose child was in the hospital. I had the distinct privilege of knowing how those people were feeling and I wanted to be on the helping end. I was feeling bad about being on the receiving end of so many completely undeserved blessings. It helped to remember that it was all to benefit Allie; she was completely innocent in all of this. She needed this and that helped me take those things that people donated to me; but I still longed to be the giver, the blessing, their angel on the planet. Despite my request, that I take the leave without pay, my friends and colleagues again came to my rescue and covered my leave entirely. I was completely grateful as we were looking at a significant amount of money that would have been taken out of my check. I was hopeful however that this would be the last time they would have to do that for me. I really wanted to be able to do it for them.

We spent the evening snacking on chocolate eggs and marshmallow peeps and contacting everyone we knew to update them on what was going to happen in the next couple of weeks for Allie. We recruited our prayer warriors nationwide and spent much time in prayer ourselves. Already we felt better, re-charged from the prayers of our friends and family. We found some fun things to do throughout the week before her surgery the following Thursday. We actually found a local junior zoo that was located right next to a playground free to the public. It was so much fun. Allie had a blast playing with the equipment that showed various energy saving things and she absolutely loved looking at all the animals. The junior zoo had a limited showing of animals but it was free and we easily found ourselves there for a couple of hours. They had a peacock, and a leopard, as well as a starfish, turtle and a couple of rabbits. We then moved ourselves outside to play on the playground. She found a little friend and they chased each other around the slide and pushed each other on the swings. Again, we got to pretend we were normal for a while, just a couple of folks bringing a kid to the park to play.

We scheduled her MRI so that she would not have to have any sedation. Apparently, my letter had made a difference. The hospital was now equipped with the headphones and movie gear that I knew would allow Allie to be without sedation for her MRIs. I was ecstatic at this new change and was hopeful that we would see some more. I crunched the numbers and found that she had eleven MRIs, four CT scans, three EEG studies, three nuclear medicine studies with Diamox, four brain arteriograms and was going on her fourth brain surgery in the three years. At this point, anything they could do to get rid of sedation at any of these points was a step in the right direction.

Allie did great throughout the MRI, no sedation and no problems whatsoever. The next day we arrived ready for our nuclear blood flow study with and without Diamox. They would do the flow study without Diamox first, then inject the Diamox and scan that by CT two hours later. The entire procedure took about four hours with two CT scans of her brain, one with Diamox and one without. In the meantime, Allie and I slept side by side on a hospital bed in a darkened room. This was all part of the process, as she needed to either be sedated, or sleep before they scanned her brain. Neither one of us had any trouble sleeping lying down and snuggling so this was an easy test for her. Again, we were able to do it without sedation and so she was able to eat before and immediately afterward. This was a tremendous blessing for us. There was nothing more troubling than to see my baby girl hungry and grumpy, even if it was only for a few hours. I was relieved that she had done so well and we went out to lunch immediately after the procedure.

The next day was Wednesday and Allie needed her blood drawn for surgery the following day. I remember, she hated having her blood drawn and she kept putting her hands behind her back and saying, "I hate hospitals." I couldn't have agreed more but we had to do it none the less. Eventually, she stopped resisting and placed her arm up there for them to draw blood. She had countless blood draws on the Coumadin, it had become completely routine for her and I reminded her of that fact when she was resisting. We left the hospital that day trying to enjoy the last day before her brain surgery. I needed some serious prayers for courage this time. I knew what to expect and I wasn't comforted by it. I was actually very stressed about the stay, particularly in the PICU where we had such a bad experience the first few times.

Thursday morning came and we stocked up on popsicles for the occasion. Her surgery was scheduled for 1:00 p.m. and she could have clear liquids and popsicles until 10:00 a.m. She ate a couple of bites off the popsicle but was completely uninterested. She asked for spaghetti-ohs to which I again had to reply, "After they fix brainy for you."

She replied with "Awww dang it." She wasn't at all excited about the prospect of having brainy fixed again. She had been through that three times previously and none of them were any fun. I could feel her apprehension and I immediately called on my prayer warriors. I had several friends and family members who were in prayer for us and that I had promised to call as soon as the procedure was over. We brought her up to the hospital and checked her in, only to find that her surgery had been moved to 2:00 p.m. Hopeful that this would be the last time we had to do this, we proceeded to the Ford Family Surgery Center. We checked in and at about 3:00 p.m. they finally took her back to be sedated. I gave her a big kiss on the forehead and a big hug. I told her I would be there when she woke up. Dad and I hadn't eaten all day and so we made our way to the hospital cafeteria again. I was so tired of doing this over and over again and was very quiet and deep in thought in the hospital cafeteria. I was praying while I was thinking about things. I kept wondering if I had made the right decision. Was this surgery going to be her last, or might we be doing this again in another year? I did not want to think about ever having to do this again and I knew in my heart that we were right where God wanted us to be. It was just so hard to watch her go through this time after time and I was frankly getting very tired of leaning so hard on everyone for everything. I just wanted everything to be okay from here on out, I wanted Allie to be healed of this condition, to be free of it. I would go from being angry to being thankful that she was still with us. I felt guilty when I got angry. "Why us?" always turned to "why not us?" Other people in the hospital were there with much more grueling problems. Those parents were watching their children suffer as well. Several times I had looked up and pleaded with God to "beam me up!" I was exhausted and the hospital stay was only just beginning.

Our favorite surgical nurse came out to tell us that they had just gotten started around 6:00 p.m. At 9:00 p.m., she gave us a report that he was finished and they were closing. She said that Dr. Steinberg would be in to talk to us any minute. Finally, Dr. Steinberg arrived and told me what I was hoping to hear; everything had gone well. He did say that he used as much of the dura as he could, as it would be her last surgery. He stated, he would not be doing another surgery on her, this was it. He said, he felt optimistic, but could not guarantee that this would fix it. And so, a flood of emotions overwhelmed me. I was thankful that things had gone well. I was terrified that this was the last surgery he would do for her. If this didn't work, we were stuck with what we had. She could possibly be doomed to a life of TIA activity throughout the day that would not allow her any type of normalcy in her life. I was thankful that they got my dad and me to see her when they did. I was tired and I needed to see my baby girl.

We met her up in the PICU, thankful that the nurse who was assigned to us wasn't Edith. They had shaved Allie's head in a one and one half inch wide spread from the top of her left ear across the midline of the top of her head. The sutures were covered by a gauze bandage that was taped down onto the hair on her head. She was sleeping and had an IV in her left arm and an arterial line under her right arm. She also was sporting a catheter. The catheter and arterial line were new. They didn't have those on her last time. I knew she would hate the catheter and being unable to use either arm wasn't going to go over well either. I just sat there with her, stroked her face and told her I loved her and that mommy is here. They gave her pain medicine which knocked her out enough that she wasn't even asking for food. I was thankful, because I knew the entire food process would be a nightmare and she hadn't eaten anything except a couple of popsicle bites this morning. It was late and my dad gave her a kiss and left knowing she was in good hands. He promised to be back in the morning. I told him not to bring me anything for breakfast, just in case she still wasn't able to eat. I made an effort to tell our nurse that there was a certain nurse we could not have. I said her name and the nurse immediately knew who I was talking about. She went to the desk and made a note in her chart. They didn't bother to even assign me a bed space but instead brought me a blanket and a pillow and told me I was welcome to stay with her overnight. I felt an absolute wave of relief. They had heard me. They had read the letter and responded by allowing me to stay with my baby girl in the PICU overnight. They never told me I couldn't use my cell phone, and made an effort to tell me that I was welcome to participate in report. Report was the time when the attending nurse filled the upcoming shift nurse in on Allie. I wasn't allowed anywhere near the nurses during report last time so this was a huge change. I felt the hand of God on us and knew at once that everything was going to be okay. I was at complete peace and there was no one capable of giving me that feeling except for the Lord God Himself. I slept in my chair next to my baby girl and waited for the sun to rise.

Allie awoke the next morning with a headache and they immediately gave her more pain medicine. They also wanted to remove the catheter and I was sure that would be a fun time. They had ordered an MRI and wanted to make sure she had nothing to eat or drink until after the MRI. I was thankful that she wasn't feeling good, because it meant she wouldn't be screaming for food any time soon. The pain medicine kept her sleeping most of the day and I was extremely grateful for that. We were moved to general population later that day, waiting patiently for a room on the floor. General population wasn't too bad, although our particular nurse was absent for the most part. They allowed clear liquids and jello when she was awake and also wanted to remove her arterial line. I was thankful for the catheter being gone and the arterial line being gone because I knew it meant we were one step closer to being out of the hospital. I remember her MRI kept getting moved later and later until it was almost midnight when we were wheeled into the room. It was during report that they had made mention of her sedation for the MRI. I interjected that she didn't have to be sedated for it because she hadn't been sedated for the last one they had done on her. They were intrigued when I told them that a movie was all she needed. They were instantly ready to move on that one and decided she didn't need sedation. That was just one more argument for parents being allowed to participate in report. She didn't need sedation but they still limited her to clear liquids. Apparently the dye they put into the IV during the MRI can make a patient nauseated to the point of throwing up. They were fairly sure they didn't need a post-brain surgery patient throwing up anywhere, much less in the MRI machine with her headphones on and no way to move any part of her body. We walked to the MRI room and on the way we were told by the nurse that they were getting her a room on the floor. I was so excited. Another complete and total answer to prayer, once again. Inside the MRI room, I was given my earplugs and Allie picked a movie from the list. She was tucked in nicely and the MRI machine started just after midnight. I sat with her and watched the machine go back and forth and around her head and body. Forty-five minutes passed and they brought in the dye to inject in her arm. I held her hand while the medicine went in and soon the nurse was grabbing Allie trying to sit her up. She was vomiting from the medicine they had injected in her IV. They said this could happen, but I couldn't believe it was happening. Allie was dripping with sweat from the MRI machine and all of the heat it put off. She had an awful look on her face. She hadn't had anything to eat so whatever she was vomiting must have been extremely foul. She looked as if she was choking on it and I just kept looking at her and telling her she was okay. Her eyes were huge as she looked at me and I instantly realized that no sedative may have been a mistake. She swallowed whatever was in her mouth, looked at me and started to cry. I just held her and told her it was okay. The nurses said, "She only has three more minutes left, do you think she can do it?" I asked her and of course she shook her head no very absolutely. I told her she could do it and I said I would be right beside her the entire time. Bravely Allie lay back down, let them strap her in and commenced to finishing the MRI. It was the longest three minutes ever, but she did it. She did it, and I was determined I would never ask her to do anything like that ever again. I was at the verge of tears but knew that I could not break down in front of her. We gathered our things and walked to our room on the floor where we would spend the duration of our stay. Allie was way too tired to eat as it was nearing 2:00 a.m. so we just watched a little television and fell asleep.

The next morning Allie got breakfast in bed, her favorite part of being in the hospital, if there can be a favorite part. She began getting quickly annoyed by the IV still in her arm, still hooked to the IV fluids going into her. They had removed the machines that were monitoring her O2 sats, heart rate and blood pressure which meant we were just that much closer to being released. The social worker came by to let us know that the playroom would be open that day and that Allie was welcome to come in and play from 2-4 p.m. Allie was ecstatic. The other thing that Allie loved about being in the hospital was the playrooms. The playrooms were staffed with volunteers and lots of toys. This particular day, they were using fuse beads. Allie loved fuse beads but they were extremely difficult with the IV in her left hand. Allie was completely left-handed from the stroke and she was having a great deal of difficulty using her left hand with an IV in it. She persevered as always and was able to do two different fuse bead projects. Grandpa Chuck and I helped her a little and she even got to play in the sensory table that was filled completely with colored rice. They had already removed the bandage over her sutures and so she was left with a nice big shaved area that showed a swollen, red suture line with large black stitches. It saddened me because her hair had just started growing in from the last surgery but at least she was playing. She was doing really well, but she tired easily. She was still getting painkillers in her IV but was going home on liquid Tylenol. She had always done well on that and I was hopeful this would be no different.

We spent one more night in the hospital, and finally were released to go back to my dad's motor home. Once there, we rested and relaxed, so happy to finally be done with yet another hospital and brain surgery. Allie looked great, but she was desperately in need of a bath. The motor home offered only a shower, so a shower it was. It was amazing how different she looked after the shower; she was like a brand new child. That brand new child would not stop bugging us about finding a beach; it was literally all she could talk about. My dad and I got on-line and found a beach only thirty minutes away. Half-Moon Bay was a beach that looked awesome, but it was certainly one we had never been to in our trips to Palo Alto. We stopped on the way to gather Allie a hat. We felt the benefits of a hat were two fold, one it would cover the terrible scar that was covering most of her head and two, it would keep the sun off of her face and prevent a painful burn. It turned out, Allie loved her new hello kitty hat and she wore it wherever we went. I was thankful, because I wasn't completely sure what other people might say if they saw her new scars.

We made it to Half-Moon Bay beach and it was as if Allie was completely at home. She loved the waves and played in the sand. She spent a great deal of time going up and down the sandy beach looking for sea shells or special rocks. The weather was perfect and warm and the water wasn't freezing like it had been before. Allie could have stayed all day, had we let her. There wasn't a place to grab a snack or a drink and so we could only stay there so long. It was more like a park, not at all like the boardwalk, but we loved it. We had brought some snacks to tide us over but about four hours in, we were too hungry to stay any longer. Allie cried and cried and at first refused to walk to the car. Eventually, she caved but she asked over and over again could she come back tomorrow. As much as I loved taking her to the beach and having her enjoy it, I was still a little afraid of doing too much, pushing her too hard.

The next day, instead of the beach, we felt like a nice relaxing movie might be in order. There was a nice downtown Palo Alto theater with a huge escalator, one of Allie's favorite things. We then got to go to a used bookstore that my dad had found before we got there. It was the neatest thing. Allie picked the "Chika Chika Boom Boom" book and read it over and over again in the car.

Wednesday morning, we prepared to see Dr. Steinberg and hopefully get released to fly back home to our family. Allie missed her daddy and her brothers and sister terribly. There were times that if we talked about them, she would cry. Needless to say, we didn't talk about them very much, it only caused both of us pain. We arrived and Dr. Steinberg's nurse checked us out. She stated that Allie would not be able to participate in PE or Soccer for four more weeks. Allie was pretty irritated by that, she loved playing soccer. I asked several questions about the future. I needed to know what I could expect from this point forward. I needed to know, what to do if this happened again. The nurse confirmed what Dr. Steinberg had said. This was Allie's last brain surgery; he would not do another one on her. If the TIA's started back up again she wanted us to call, but they would be looking at possibly starting her on anti-seizure medication. This did not sound promising. I knew, as they did, these were not seizures but in essence there was nothing more they could do for her. We had exhausted our last medical hope. I breathed a deep sigh and right then and there gave it all to God. I had done everything I could for her, they had done everything they could for her and in a way it was a relief. But in another way, the prospect of being helpless has its own worry.

I try not to think about it, even now. It makes me sick to my stomach to think that in a year's time, we could be having a TIA every four hours and there will be nothing they can do for us. It also gives me pause to think that perhaps, nothing else will be needed. Allie will be okay, just the way she is; she is a blessing and a gift. Allie has been my little perspective keeper. She has amazed me with her constant smile, her strength and her unending sweetness. I don't know what her future holds, but I know ultimately God holds her future. It's in His hands. I am a realist and I can accept it if God calls her home. Believe me when I say, I would much rather have her here with me, but I am extremely thankful that God has allowed me to be her mother for these last seven years. God had shown me the kind of person, the kind of mother and the kind of advocate that I could be for my children. He allowed me to experience something that was both inspiring and terrifying. And through it all, I felt His presence with us and I saw the many, unending gifts and blessings that He bestowed upon us. God is good and we are blessed.

For God so loved the world, that he gave his only Son, that whoever believes in him should not perish but have eternal life. John 3:16

EPILOGUE

—⁘—

As of this writing, I have been living in our small rural town, taking care of my four children as best I can. Brennan is in the eighth grade and is getting ready to graduate from our small rural school and must choose a high school to finish through twelfth grade. Our school is Pre-K through eighth grade only. He has continued to do well in school with only a few setbacks. His medicine works well for him until about 2:00 p.m. in school so last hour is a little rough for him. He has encountered his first really challenging teacher, not bad to go that many years without one. She definitely has given him much grief this year. Between making fun of his small stature by calling him "little man", and assigning homework every day, it has been a rough haul for both him and me. He continues to referee for our local church athletic group and has officiated both football and basketball. He absolutely loves it. In fact, my father-in-law bought him a referee shirt for Christmas, so he could be official. He turned fourteen last week and it is hard for me to believe. He is still, most days, very compassionate and helpful, loving and kind to his sisters. He is still at odds with his brother who continues to outgrow him and continues to be uninterested in playing sports. Brennan envies his brother's tallness and athletic prowess and doesn't understand the cruel joke of autism, which has made his brother completely uninterested in sports. He now has his own Facebook page and Ipod, which I must monitor frequently for inappropriate content. His health has been excellent and despite his unkempt room, he has taken to wearing cologne and taking showers daily, something I wasn't sure would ever happen.

Adam is now in the fourth grade and turned eleven in January. He continues to grow, and his shoe size is now larger than his fathers. He struggles with writing in cursive for the most part in school. He has an amazing teacher this year who loves him for who he is and totally gets his humor. He continues to be completely interested in Lego and Ninjago as well as Mario. We got him a Nintendo DS for Christmas, which he enjoys playing Mario games on. He has a unique set up in his room currently which involves cardboard boxes he has turned into a mall of sort for his Lego people and dinosaurs to enjoy. Each piece has a place and if out of place, incurs the wrath of Adam, so to speak. He continues to wear the same shirt and pants every day, despite my efforts to buy him multiple copies of the same shirt and pants. He just prefers not to have to start over, I imagine. He has become interested in the show "Doomsday Preppers" and on any given day, you can find him in the field, digging his shelter and planning what to pack in his "bug-out" bag should the end of the world come too soon. He invited the same two boys to his birthday party in January that he has invited for the last seven years. They came to the party and enjoyed time together swimming at the local recreation center. He has confided in me that he prays every night that God will come into his heart, a revelation I am very proud of. I told him he need only ask once and God will come right in. He smiled at me when I said it almost like he wasn't quite sure I was telling the truth. We have started him in speech outside of school so he can get one-on-one help with social scripts and reading social cues. This brings our outside therapy total to about $160 per week for everything. He really needs to have OT out of school as well but that would put us a little over the budget. He continues to sleep in and hates brushing his teeth. We have started some medication for him to help him focus on his work while he is at school. He seems to like it, although, he is physically unable to swallow a pill. Apparently, oral apraxia makes it impossible for him to steady the pill on the back of his tongue so that he can swallow it. I watched him struggle several times as he lost the pill within his mouth, got it stuck between his check and his teeth and was unable to retrieve it with his tongue. His doctor prescribed a capsule which can be opened into his chocolate milk, so that he doesn't have to keep chewing a non-chewable medication. The first day, his teacher noticed a dramatic improvement. He had been doing nothing in class and was bringing home a ridiculous amount of work. Adam's homework always took us literally over two hours a night to do. On the medicine, he finishes his work at school. We also have written in his IEP the modification that he only have to write in cursive on his spelling work, this helps him to be able to concentrate on his creative writing assignments, rather than get lost in the cursive writing.

Emma is in the first grade this year, the same class as her sister Allie. Emma continues to be very petite and for a time, was taking the growth hormone shots. She has since decided to just be small because the shots in her bottom hurt way too much. She continues to have trouble with anxiety and had a panic attack the night of Allie's eye surgery. She started hyperventilating and I had to take her to the emergency room. She doesn't like for me to leave for long periods and continues to sleep with me at night. She hasn't given up on her dream to become a singer and wants to take singing lessons as soon as possible. She starred in the Christmas Play the first grade puts on at our school when she and Allie sang "Happy Birthday Jesus" to the baby in the manger. She is doing very well in school and is an above average reader in her grade. She loves to read. She has taken to covering her ears with her hair as apparently someone in her class told her she had pointy ears. She is quite the fancy dresser and prefers sparkly and shiny dresses, to pants and t-shirts. We continue to get Speech therapy for her outside of school, as she has difficulty with word retrieval and syntax in her expressive communication. She does have a beautiful voice which I can only imagine rivals the angels in heaven and I have taken to just enjoying every second of hearing her voice in song.

I continue to teach kindergarten and this year has been the most challenging. I have 25 children in a class that was never designed for that many. I also have a new principal who has no children and who has never been in the classroom. This has proved to be extremely challenging as I try to advocate for not only my own children, but for the children who have special needs in the classroom. I am not much of a brown-noser as I seem to have completely lost my taste for it. So to say the least, I am not a favorite. I have however been nominated for an Excellence in Teaching Award. No doubt the award doesn't mean as much to me as each child who tells me they love me, or gives me a hug and tells me I'm the best teacher ever. That is why I teach. I continue to feel the need to combat wrong doing and thinking almost as if I am continuing in the war zone of the hospital environment while protecting Allie. I don't know if it is Post Traumatic Stress Syndrome from so much trauma and stress over the last four years or if it is just the new me—the no-nonsense me; the "me" that has her priorities in order and doesn't settle for "good enough". I am now a person who is revolted by gossip and despises others' quest for things over people. I am a person who loves people more than things. I am a person who will go to bat for the innocent, regardless of the consequences. Is this who God wants me to be? I still have no answers to that question. I continue on my path until he smacks me over the head with a brick and points me in a new direction, yes I am just that hardheaded.

Allie is in first grade at school and is doing the best that she can do. She continues to have problems with auditory processing which leads her to lose focus and attention frequently. She has a paraprofessional that is with her for an hour in the afternoon to help her stay focused on her math and spelling tests. She reads below average—but she reads. Reading is one miracle in and of itself. She continues to have TIA activity most of which are small and last less than five minutes. It is spring, however and spring is our "TIA season", others have soccer and baseball season—we have TIA season. She was hospitalized just last week for a TIA that started at school and dilated her eyes making it impossible for her to see her work. I of course was not there as I was taking Adam to the orthopedist in Tulsa. Her teacher was completely beside herself and she was worried sick about her. The TIA lasted more than 36 hours and during that time, we were admitted to Saint Francis in Tulsa for an MRI with and without contrast and a 24 hour video EEG. She was a trooper as usual and did the MRI without anesthesia. No new strokes were found and no seizure activity either. I have decided to put her on an allergy medicine to see if the TIA increase in activity is allergy related. Mother's intuition tells me it may just be related. Since being on the allergy medicine, she has been TIA free since her hospitalization. I forgot to give it to her just one night, and she had two episodes the next day. We are scheduled to go back to California in May for a recheck. She will have the MRI with and without contrast, two flow studies and the arteriogram while we are down there. Sometimes, I look her and I think—wow—what an amazing little girl she is. She can walk, talk, read, skip, jump, laugh and sing. Sometimes, I look at her and think, "What is her potential? How much longer will I have her? What does her future hold?" I don't know what her future holds, but I know who holds her future. It is in those words I cling to peace for as long as I can, until the day that my world is again shaken. I know that whatever happens, God is with us every step of the way. It is only through Him that we have the strength to get up in the morning, to see each day and embrace it. It is through Him that we can be thankful for those experiences that make us who we are, good or bad, they are of His design. Only He can see the bigger picture.

As my dad exited the Walmart last Monday, during one of the worst wind and rain storms this year, he opened his umbrella only to have it blow away along with his favorite Texas cowboy hat. As he ran to catch the umbrella, he became more drenched with the cold rain and lost his cart full of groceries. The groceries, some for himself, and some for me, were headed for the parking lot at full speed. As he ran to try to keep up with them, his recent weight loss combined with the heavy wetness from the rain caused him to almost lose his pants. He watched as the cart did a flip and groceries flew everywhere. His Kleenex was ruined and my milk had exploded all over the other groceries. As he told me this story, I began to think of my life. It was a metaphor indeed. If you focus on the things that matter the least, you stand to lose all that is most important to you. My faith in God has carried me through the mightiest of storms. We still have cloudy days and there may be another storm on the horizon, but I have my Almighty God to watch over me and my family. We are blessed.

> *Yea, though I walk through the valley of the shadow of death, I will fear no evil: for thou art with me; thy rod and thy staff they comfort me.*
> *Thou preparest a table before me in the presence of mine enemies: thou anointest my head with oil; my cup runneth over. Surely goodness and mercy shall follow me all the days of my life: and I will dwell in the house of the LORD for ever. Psalm 23:4–6*

CPSIA information can be obtained at www.ICGtesting.com
Printed in the USA
LVOW121052290912

300785LV00003B/2/P